Science 4 Today

Grade 6

by
Margaret Fetty

Frank Schaffer Publications®

Author: Margaret Fetty
Editor: Nathan Hemmelgarn

Frank Schaffer Publications®

Send all inquiries to:
Frank Schaffer Publications
8720 Orion Place
Columbus, Ohio 43240-2111

Science 4 Today—grade 6

ISBN: 0-7682-3526-X

2 3 4 5 6 7 8 9 10 POH 12 11 10 09 08

Table of Contents

Science and Technology

Science in Personal and Social Perspectives

History and the Nature of Science

What Is Science 4 Today?

Science 4 Today is a comprehensive yet quick and easy-to-use supplement designed to complement any science curriculum. Based on the National Science Education Standards (NSES), forty topics cover essential concepts that sixth-grade students should understand and know in natural science. During the course of four days, presumably Monday through Thursday, students complete questions and activities focusing on each topic in about ten minutes. On the fifth day, students complete a twenty-minute assessment to practice test-taking skills, including multiple choice, true-false, and short answer.

How Does It work?

Unlike many science programs, *Science 4 Today* adopts the eight major standards outlined by the NSES to ascertain students' science skills. The standards are:

- unifying concepts and processes in science.
- science as inquiry.
- physical science.
- life science.
- Earth and space science.
- science and technology.
- science in personal and social perspectives.
- history and nature of science.

The book supplies forty topics commonly found in the sixth-grade science curriculum. Educators can choose a topic confident that it will support their unit of study and at least one of the eight standards. The Skills and Concepts chart on pages 8–10 identifies the main concepts for each week to insure that the content aligns with the classroom topic. The Scope and Sequence chart further supports identifying the specific skills following the standards. The answer key, found on pages 93–112, is provided for both daily activities and general assessments.

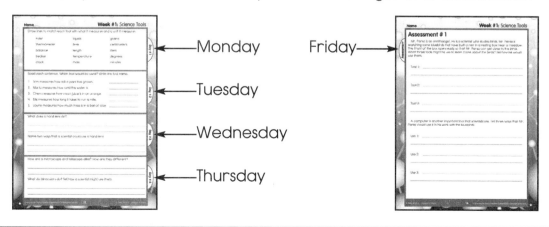

How Was It Developed?

Science 4 Today was created in response to a need to assess students' understanding of important science concepts. Basals teach the necessary skills, but might not apply them to other overarching standards outlined by the NSES. Moreover, with the increased emphasis on standardized testing, the necessity for experience with test styles and semantics also becomes apparent.

How Can It Be Used?

Science 4 Today can be easily implemented into the daily routine of the classroom, depending on your teaching style. The activities and questions can be written on the board each day, or the whole page can be copied on a transparency and displayed at the appropriate time. It is also possible to copy the weekly page as a blackline master and distribute it at the beginning of each week. Students can complete the activities during attendance or other designated time. After completion, the class can briefly check and discuss the assignment.

What Are the Benefits?

The daily approach of *Science 4 Today* provides reading comprehension practice in science, higher-level thinking exercises, and problem-solving strategies. The pages also target test-taking skills by incorporating the style and syntax of standardized tests. Because of its consistent format, *Science 4 Today* not only offers opportunities for instruction but also serves as an excellent diagnostic tool.

Test-Taking Tips

Short Answer Questions

- Read the directions carefully. Be sure you know what you are expected to do. Ask questions if you do not understand.

- Read the whole question before you answer it. Some questions might have multiple parts.

- If you do not know the answer right away, come back to it after completing the other items.

- Review each question and answer after completing the whole test. Does your answer make sense? Does it answer the whole question?

- Check for spelling, punctuation, and grammar mistakes.

Multiple Choice Questions

- Read the question before looking at the answers. Then, come up with the answer in your head before looking at the choices to avoid confusion.

- Read all the answers before choosing the best answer.

- Eliminate answers that you know are not correct.

- Fill in the whole circle. Do not mark outside the circle.

- Review the questions and your answers after completing the whole test. Your first response is usually correct unless you did not read the question correctly.

True – False Questions

- Read each statement carefully. Look at the key words to understand the statement.

- Look at the qualifying words. Words like *all*, *always*, and *never* often signal a false statement. General words, like *sometimes*, *often*, and *usually*, most likely signal a true statement.

- If any part of the statement is false, the whole statement is false.

Skills and Concepts

Scope and Sequence

Skills/Concepts	1	2	3	4	5	6	7	8	9	10	11	12	13	14	15	16	17	18	19	20	21	22	23	24	25	26	27	28	29	30	31	32	33	34	35	36	37	38	39	40
Unifying Concepts and Processes in Science																																								
Systems			•																																					
Order and organization		•							•			•				•					•				•															
Measuring			•								•											•																		
Graphic aids			•	•		•	•			•	•								•			•			•									•						
Science as Inquiry																																								
Science process skills	•	•			•																			•	•	•			•					•	•	•				
Scientific method		•	•		•																					•														
Science inquiry			•	•																				•	•		•								•	•				
Physical Science																																								
Elements and atoms						•	•			•																														
Properties of matter						•	•			•																														
Motion								•										•	•	•	•		•												•					•
Energy									•		•														•															
Properties of sound									•	•																														
Properties of light											•														•										•					
Life Science																																								
Cells												•	•	•		•										•														
Heredity and genetics													•													•														
Populations														•																							•	•		
Diversity and adaptations												•			•	•																								
Plants														•	•	•																								
Animal behavior																	•																			•				
Earth and Space Science																																								
Solar system																		•	•	•				•																

• Indicates Skill or Concept Included

Published by Frank Schaffer Publications. Copyright protected.   0-7682-3526-X   *Science 4 Today*

Scope and Sequence

Skills/Concepts	1	2	3	4	5	6	7	8	9	10	11	12	13	14	15	16	17	18	19	20	21	22	23	24	25	26	27	28	29	30	31	32	33	34	35	36	37	38	39	40
Moon																			●																					
Hydrosphere																				●																				
Atmosphere																					●																			
Climate																						●																		
Shaping Earth																							●															●		
Science and Technology																																								
NASA's contributions																								●																
Microscopes																									●															
Forensic science																										●												●		
Science in careers																											●													
Computers																												●												
Science in Personal and Social Perspectives												●																	●	●	●	●	●							
Body systems												●																	●	●	●	●	●							
Emotions																														●										
Healthy lifestyles										●																				●	●		●							
Drugs and alcohol																																●								
Diseases																																	●							
Recycling																																		●			●			
History and Nature of Science					●			●																											●	●				
Famous scientists					●			●																											●	●				
Smart animals																																				●				
Conservation																				●	●													●			●			
Missing populations																																						●		
Money																																							●	
Native Americans																																								●

● Indicates Skill or Concept Included

Read each sentence. Write the name of the science process skill described.

1. Alma uses her senses to learn about the color, shape, and smell of the flower. _____

2. Ben looks at the numbers on the spring scale to discover how much force is needed to move the toy car up the ramp. _____

3. Asa groups her rock collection by their process of formation. _____

4. Since Tom is opening a can of cat food, he expects to see his cat. She comes running any time she hears the can opener. _____

5. Ella and Max talk about the results of their lab experiment. _____

6. The nighttime sky was very dark even though there were no clouds. Mark knew that the moon would wax in the next two weeks. _____

What is the difference in an observation and an inference?

_____

_____

Why are measurements important to scientists? Give three reasons.

_____

_____

_____

Look at the list of items in the box. Classify them into groups. Label the groups.

| frog | bluebird | sapphires | lion | grass | elephant | sun | car |

Classify each group again. Label the groups.

What are three ways that scientists communicate?

_____

_____

_____

What are three kinds of graphic aids? Why do scientists use graphic aids?

_____

_____

Assessment # 1

Read the paragraph. Then, answer the questions.

Maria is doing an experiment about the best kind of insulating material. She fills a jar with hot water, measures the temperature, and records it in a chart. After tightly screwing on the lid, Maria puts the jar in a box filled with wool material. She checks the temperature of the water after 30 minutes, recording it in the chart. Maria repeats the experiment three more times, using the same water temperature with plastic wrap, foil, and air insulations. Maria looks at her chart and sees that the water temperature stayed the warmest in the wool. Maria decides that the wool is the best insulator.

1. Identify and explain three science process skills that Maria uses.

_____

_____

2. What operational definition could Maria make for the word *insulation*?

_____

_____

3. How did Maria use the measurements to make an inference?

_____

_____

Fill in the circle next to the best answer.

4. Which sense did Maria use the most during her experiment?

   (A) hearing   (C) smell

   (B) sight   (D) touch

5. What would be the best way for Maria to record her measurements?

   (A) circle graph   (C) bar graph

   (B) line graph   (D) diagram

Write numbers **1** through **8** to show the steps of the scientific method.

_____ Interpret the data

_____ Investigate further

_____ Plan the experiment and the variables

_____ State the problem

_____ Test the hypothesis

_____ Collect the data

_____ Communicate the conclusion

_____ Formulate a hypothesis

Name two reasons telling why scientists follow the scientific method.

_____

_____

Jason has three foods—potato chips, an apple, and a nutrition bar. He wants to plan an experiment to find out which has the most fat. What hypothesis can Jason make?

_____

What is a theory?

_____

_____

How is a theory different from a law?

_____

_____

The ancient Greek scientist Ptolemy said that the sun revolved around Earth. This theory was believed for many centuries. In the 1500s, Copernicus announced a new theory, which said Earth moved around the sun. Most people did not believe it until Galileo used a telescope, a new invention, to see large bodies circling in a path around Jupiter. With the help of mathematical equations formulated by other scientists, Copernicus' idea was proven and became a law.

What are two reasons that theories are disproved?

_____

_____

Assessment # 2

Answer the questions.

1. What is the correct order in the scientific process? Write numbers
   1 through **5**.

   _____ theory

   _____ hypothesis

   _____ question

   _____ law

   _____ experiment

2. Why does it take so long for scientists to agree on a scientific law?

   _____

3. Read the statement below. Identify what part of the scientific process it is.
   Explain how you know.

   An object will remain in motion or stay at rest until a force acts on it.

   _____

   _____

Fill in the circle next to the best answer.

4. What will a scientist most likely do if the hypothesis and conclusion do not
   match?

   (A) Identify the hypothesis as a theory.   (C) State a new hypothesis.

   (B) Communicate the results with the   (D) Give up because the
       scientific community.   hypothesis was wrong.

5. Which of the following is the best hypothesis?

   (A) Which flower color attracts bees   (C) The red flowers are
       the most?   the prettiest.

   (B) Hummingbirds visit bright-colored   (D) Bees work harder than
       flowers more than pale-colored   hummingbirds.
       flowers.

Complete the chart to tell corresponding units used to measure each characteristic.

Characteristic	Standard Units	Metric Units
Mass		
Liquid Capacity		
Length		
Distance		
Temperature		

What measurement system is used in the science community?

_____

Why do all scientists use this system?

_____

_____

_____

How is a bar graph like a line graph? How are they different?

_____

_____

What kind of graph would a food nutritionist use to show the percentage of ingredients in a glass of lemonade? Why?

_____

_____

_____

List five important tools commonly used by scientists in all fields and explain their uses.

_____

_____

_____

_____

_____

Assessment

Assessment # 3

Complete the page.

1. Choose a device, such as a computer, cell phone, or television. Draw and label a diagram to show its parts.

2. Laura helped a park ranger count the number of trees in an acre. She recorded it in the chart below. Draw a graph to show the data.

Trees	Number
Pine	28
Oak	11
Maple	3

3. Explain why you chose the kind of graph above.

_____

_____

4. Give two reasons explaining why a scientist maintains detailed records while doing research?

_____

_____

Fill in the circle next to the best answer.

5. Which tool would be used to measure a small amount of liquid for an experiment?

   (A) a crucible   (C) a graduated cylinder

   (B) a beaker   (D) a Petri dish

Write *true* or *false*.

1. _____ An experiment always tests a hypothesis.

2. _____ A scientist makes a prediction based on the results of the experiment.

3. _____ Experiments need to be controlled to make sure they are fair.

4. _____ It is important to change at least two variables during an experiment.

5. _____ All data needs to be carefully recorded during an experiment.

Use each word in a sentence to explain its meaning.

dependent variable: _____

_____

independent variable: _____

_____

controlled variable: _____

_____

Write **S** in front of each rule that shows a safe lab practice.

_____ Wear safety glasses when you are working with glass, heat, or chemicals.

_____ Dispose of all liquids in the lab sink when you are done.

_____ Look down into the opening of a heating container to watch the reaction.

_____ Wash your hands before and after conducting a lab experiment.

_____ Baggy clothes should be avoided on lab days.

_____ Place heated glassware into cool water immediately to easily remove residue.

_____ Horsing around should be avoided.

Should you read the entire set of instructions before beginning an experiment? Why or why not?

_____

_____

_____

_____

_____

Assessment # 4

Complete the page.

1. Sam noticed that a bronze statue in the park was turning green. He wants to find out why. What should Sam do before stating a hypothesis?

_____

_____

_____

_____

2. In planning the experiment, what three materials might Sam need?

_____

_____

_____

3. Describe an experiment Sam can do to find out why the bronze statue is changing color.

_____

_____

_____

_____

_____

_____

4. What is the variable in the experiment?

_____

Unscramble the letters in bold to tell the characteristics of a good scientist.

1. Scientists need to be **sruicuo** and ask questions about things they do not understand.

2. They need to be **nitpate** and take their time when conducting an investigation.

3. When they see a problem, they need to think of **evitaerc** ways to solve it.

4. If scientists don't get the answer they want, they should be **tespitrens** and keep trying until they are successful.

5. The **sravnoteb** scientist will notice all the changes and record the notes carefully.

Day #1

Does a scientist need good math skills? Why or why not?

_____

_____

_____

How would a failure in an experiment help a scientist?

_____

_____

Day #2

Why do scientists keep notebooks or journals?

_____

What are three pieces of information scientists would include in the notebooks? Why?

_____

_____

_____

Day #3

Think about your personality. Would you make a good scientist? Explain. Give two examples to support your opinion.

_____

_____

_____

_____

Day #4

Assessment

Assessment # 5

Read the paragraph. Then, answer the question.

Jane Goodall is best known for her work with chimpanzees. She spent many years in Africa observing the behaviors of these animals. She often sat in the forests with her notebook and recorded what the animals ate, how they moved, and how they interacted with each other. She also filmed the chimpanzees as further proof of their behaviors. Later, Goodall traveled around the world telling people about her discoveries. She also actively worked to protect chimpanzees when the population became threatened due to loss of their habitat and capture.

1. Why was Jane Goodall a good scientist? Write a paragraph explaining three characteristics.

_____

_____

_____

_____

_____

_____

2. What are two ways that communication can help a scientist?

_____

_____

Fill in the circle next to the best answer.

3. What will a good scientist do?

   (A) take careful notes

   (B) conduct one experiment to prove a hypothesis

   (C) record data at the end of an experiment

   (D) share only the data that supports his hypothesis

Write *true* or *false*.

1. _____ A molecule is anything that has mass and takes up space.
2. _____ Everything in the world is made up of just 111 elements.
3. _____ Elements cannot be broken down by heat, light, or electricity.
4. _____ Only the same kind of elements can be combined.
5. _____ Elements are used to make atoms.
6. _____ The periodic table groups elements that have similar characteristics.

Day #1

Label the atom. Identify the charge of each part.

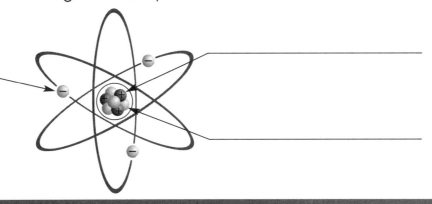

Day #2

Unscramble the letters in bold to make a word that relates to atoms.

1. Atoms from the same element that have a different number of neutrons are called **spoosite**.
2. Atoms from the same element that have a different number of electrons are called **nois**.
3. The atom's **stroncele** orbit in shells.
4. Atoms that give or receive electrons form **telavecltrone** bonds.
5. Atoms that share electrons make **lancovet** bonds.

Day #3

What does the atomic number in the periodic table tell?

_____

What are the rows called in the periodic table? How are the elements in the same row alike?

_____

What are the columns called? How are elements in the same column alike?

_____

Day #4

Assessment

Assessment # 6

Fill in the circle next to the best answer.

1. Which is not a group of elements?
   - (A) metals
   - (B) oxygen
   - (C) halogens
   - (D) sodiums

2. How many elements are there?
   - (A) about 10
   - (B) about 100
   - (C) about 1,000
   - (D) about 10,000

3. Aluminum has 13 protons. How many electrons does it have?
   - (A) 3
   - (B) 10
   - (C) 13
   - (D) not enough information

4. Which particles are inside the nucleus?
   - (A) electrons and neutrons
   - (B) protons and electrons
   - (C) neutrons and protons
   - (D) electrons and neutrons

Answer the questions.

5. Why are elements called the building blocks of matter?

_____

_____

_____

6. If you point to one element on the periodic table, what will it most likely be? Explain.

_____

_____

_____

Name

Use the words in the box to explain the diagram.

| atoms | molecule | compound |

_____

_____

The formula for rust is Fe_2O_3. Explain what each element is like. Then, explain what happens when the two elements form a compound. Draw a diagram to show a molecule.

_____

_____

_____

_____

How is a mixture the same as and different from a solution?

_____

_____

_____

Is saltwater a mixture or a solution? Explain.

_____

_____

_____

What is a physical change? Give three examples.

_____

_____

What is a chemical change? Give three examples.

_____

_____

_____

Assessment # 7

Write *true* or *false*.

1. _____ Scientists can always separate a mixture into its different parts.

2. _____ The same amount of heat is needed to change the state of all substances.

3. _____ The molecules in sawdust and a tree are the same.

4. _____ The molecules in ashes are the same as those in a tree.

5. _____ Rust is a compound.

Answer the questions.

6. What are two ways to separate a compound?

_____

_____

7. Why are no new substances made when a mixture is formed?

_____

_____

Fill in the circle next to the best answer.

8. What is true about a compound?

(A) Every molecule is the same.

(B) Most molecules are the same.

(C) Each molecule is different.

(D) It has one molecule.

9. What are bases that can be dissolved in water?

(A) acids   (C) metals

(B) alkalis   (D) salts

26

Name _____

Draw a line to match each word with its definition.

motion   the speed and direction of a moving object

speed   the distance an object moves in a given unit of time

velocity   the tendency for an object to remain at rest or in motion

acceleration   a force that pulls on and slows a moving object

inertia   a change in the position of an object as compared to a set point

friction   a force that resists the movement of one object past another

air resistance   a change in the speed or direction of a moving object

drag   friction caused when molecules in the air hit an object and slow it down

---

Lee rolled a ping-pong ball across the floor. Then, using the same force, she rolled a golf ball. Which rolled farther? Why?

_____

_____

Next, Lee holds both balls above her head so they are the same height. Which hits the ground first? Explain.

_____

Why do road crews spread sand on icy roads?

_____

_____

Why do professional bicycle riders reduce friction? Name two ways.

_____

_____

Maria has packed a large suitcase for a week-long stay with her grandmother. She has a hard time pulling it off the bed. When she gets the suitcase to the edge, it tumbles quickly to the floor. Finally, Maria drags the suitcase to the door. Explain three motion concepts affecting the suitcase.

_____

_____

_____

Assessment # 8

Answer the questions.

1. Sir Isaac Newton introduced the three laws of motion. What are they? Give an example of each.

_____

_____

_____

_____

_____

_____

_____

Fill in the circle next to the best answer.

2. Heather was walking north. She turned left and started walking west. What did Heather change?

    (A) speed

    (B) velocity

    (C) inertia

    (D) acceleration

3. A car is stopped at a light. What happens to a passenger's body when the car moves forward?

    (A) It moves forward.

    (B) It moves backward.

    (C) It doesn't move.

    (D) It moves side to side.

0-7682-3526-X   *Science 4 Today*   **28**

Write the name of the energy being described.

1. The food Rod ate powers his body. _____
2. A technician x-rays a bone to see if it is broken. _____
3. Greg turns on a lamp to read. _____
4. All the ice in the glass melts. _____
5. A power plant uses uranium to split atoms, which supplies electric energy. _____
6. Keisha takes her dog for a walk. _____
7. Soon Li listens to a band play music. _____

Day #1

Write the numbers **1** through **7** to show the order of the radiant wavelengths from shortest to longest.

_____ microwaves   _____ x-rays
_____ radio waves   _____ infrared waves
_____ visible light   _____ gamma rays
_____ ultraviolet light

What is the entire radiant wavelength called? _____

Day #2

Describe the steps used at a coal power plant to produce electricity. Name the energy change in each.

_____
_____
_____
_____
_____

Day #3

Write *true* or *false*.

1. _____ Radar guns, used by police to catch speeding cars, works with ultraviolet rays.
2. _____ All objects give off infrared waves.
3. _____ Visible light is the only form of radiant energy you can see.
4. _____ Radio waves treat cancer.
5. _____ Some televisions use radio waves.
6. _____ Visible light can cook food.
7. _____ Gamma rays can produce bacteria that harm food.

Day #4

Assessment

Assessment # 9

Answer the questions.

1. How can ultraviolet rays benefit and harm people? Give one example of each.

_____

_____

2. Name one example of each energy change.

   radiant energy to chemical energy   _____

   electric energy to mechanical energy   _____

   mechanical energy to thermal energy   _____

3. How can potential energy be changed into kinetic energy? Give one example.

_____

_____

4. How is radiant energy the same as and different from sound energy?

_____

_____

Fill in the circle next to the best answer.

5. What kind of energy is in a battery?

   (A) nuclear   (C) mechanical

   (B) radiant   (D) chemical

6. Which radiant energy wave is not dangerous?

   (A) gamma   (C) radio

   (B) x-ray   (D) ultraviolet

Draw a sound wave and label its four main parts.

What is the frequency of the sound wave that you drew? Tell how you know.

_____

_____

How is sound made? Use the words in the box in your description.

vibrations	waves	matter	molecules	source

_____

_____

_____

_____

Mitch plays a bass drum and a snare drum in the school band. Describe the pitch and loudness of each instrument. Give an explanation for each.

_____

_____

_____

Choose one musical instrument. Describe the sound it will make and why.

_____

During a thunderstorm, you might see the lightning and hear the thunder a few seconds later. Why?

_____

_____

How does the force with which someone plucks a guitar string affect its sound?

_____

_____

Assessment # 10

Look at the chart. Then, fill in the circle next to the best answer.

Animal	Approximate Range (Hz)
dog	67-45,000
human being	64-23,000
elephant	16-12,000
porpoise	75-150,000
mouse	1,000-91,000

1. Which animal can hear the highest pitched sound?

    (A) dog
    (B) elephant

    (C) human being
    (D) porpoise

2. How many vibrations must an object make for a human being to hear it?

    (A) 10
    (B) 60

    (C) 200
    (D) 24,000

3. An object is producing 38,000 Hz. Which animal cannot hear it?

    (A) mouse
    (B) elephant

    (C) porpoise
    (D) dog

Answer the questions.

4. What is compression and rarefaction in a wave? Label the diagram to show each.

_____

_____

_____

Write *true* or *false*.

1. _____ Light is given off in small particles called *photons*.
2. _____ Photons travel in waves.
3. _____ Light can move in a straight line or turn corners.
4. _____ A mirror works because of refraction.
5. _____ Reflection is where light rays are bent.
6. _____ Light can travel over 186,000 miles per second.
7. _____ White light is the same as visible light.

Day #1

Describe what is happening in the diagram.

_____

_____

_____

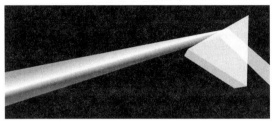

Write the order of the colors in the spectrum, from the longest to the shortest wavelength.

_____

Day #2

Circle the word that correctly completes each sentence.

1. An apple looks red because the red wavelength is (absorbed, reflected).
2. A white shirt looks white because the beam of light is (refracted, scattered).
3. Only the blue wavelength will be (absorbed, transmitted) when a blue filter covers a flashlight.
4. You can see smoke because part of the light is (transmitted, scattered) by the smoke particles, while the other part is (transmitted, scattered) through the light.
5. A curtain that is (opaque, translucent) will keep all the light from entering a room.

Day #3

What is a lens?

_____

Label each lens. Draw lines to show how light moves through them.

_____   _____

Day #4

Assessment

Assessment # 11

Answer the questions.

1. Why is a room painted with light colors brighter than a room painted with dark colors?

_____

_____

2. John knocked a pillow off the couch. Picking it up, he noticed that the side that had been facing up was lighter than the one that had been facing down. What hypothesis might John make about the color change? Describe an experiment that he can do to test his hypothesis. Be sure to include the variable he can change.

_____

_____

_____

3. Is black a color? Explain.

_____

_____

Fill in the circle next to the best answer.

4. Which is not a characteristic of visible light?

   (A) It is a form of radiant energy.   (C) It is translucent.

   (B) It produces heat.   (D) It contains some ultraviolet waves.

5. Why can you see a reflection in a mirror?

   (A) The image is reflected off a smooth surface.

   (B) The silver in the mirror conducts the image.

   (C) The glass bends the image and slows its speed.

   (D) The image scatters as it moves through the glass.

Underline the word that completes each sentence.

1. Cells are the basic units of (matter, life).
2. Cells can (reproduce, grow) by dividing.
3. The (mitochondrion, nucleus) controls the activity of the cell.
4. (Genes, Vacuoles) are found in the nucleus.
5. Before a cell divides, material in the nucleus makes a (picture, copy) of itself.
6. Cell division produces new cells that are (unlike, exactly) like the old.
7. The two new cells produced are called (daughter, parent) cells.

Day #1

Label the cell. Write one function of each part.

_____

_____

_____

_____

_____

_____

_____

_____

What is mitosis?_____

Day #2

Write numbers **1** to **4** to show the order of cell division. Write the name of each phase being described.

_____ The duplicated chromosomes line up in the center of the cell and divide. _____

_____ The chromosomes twist and thicken inside the nucleus. They duplicate and form two identical parts. The membrane around the nucleus disappears. _____

_____ A membrane forms around each set of chromosomes as they untwist. The cytoplasm divides and a new cell membrane forms around each. _____

_____ The chromosomes move to opposite sides of the cell. _____

Day #3

What are the three wastes that a cell releases?

_____

_____

Explain how the cell gets rid of these wastes in the circulatory system.

_____

_____

_____

Day #4

Assessment

Assessment # 12

Answer the questions.

1. What are the six processes of life that cells control?

_____

_____

2. Identify three specific cells in the human body. Tell what process of life they control.

_____

_____

3. Even if an organism stops growing, why are new cells constantly dividing?

_____

_____

4. Cells are the basic part the body system. What are the other parts that lead to its organization, function, and structure? List them in order from cell to body.

_____

_____

Fill in the circle next to the best answer.

5. What is another way the body gets rid of cell wastes?

   Ⓐ sodium   Ⓒ saliva

   Ⓑ sweat   Ⓓ saline

6. Which part of mitosis does the picture show?

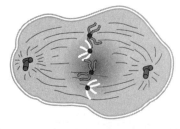

   Ⓐ prophase   Ⓒ anaphase

   Ⓑ metaphase   Ⓓ telophase

Draw a line to match each word with its definition.

heredity	a gene whose characteristic is hidden by a dominant gene
genetics	a section of the chromosome that controls a trait
inherit	the study of heredity
gene	the passing of characteristics from one generation to the next
recessive gene	a gene that can mask the characteristic of another gene
dominant gene	a feature or characteristic gotten from a parent
trait	to get a characteristic from a parent or ancestor
DNA	the pattern of chemicals in a cell that determine the life, growth, and unique features of an organism

Day #1

A guinea pig can have smooth or rough hair. Rough hair is dominant. Suppose that the letter symbol for the trait is **r**. What pairs of genes might a parent guinea pig have? Describe what the guinea pig having each of those genes would look like.

_____

_____

Two parents have rough fur. Draw Punnett squares to show what genes the offspring might inherit.

Day #2

What is a mutation?

_____

How might a mutation help a species? How might it harm a species?

_____

_____

_____

Day #3

What is selective breeding?

_____

_____

Does selective breeding benefit farmers? Why or why not?

_____

_____

Day #4

Assessment

Assessment # 13

Answer the questions.

1. How are an organism's traits controlled by its genes?

_____

_____

_____

_____

_____

2. Suppose that a rose bred to be large and fragrant, only produced white blooms. How might a plant nursery produce a rose that is large, fragrant, and red?

_____

_____

3. Genetic engineering involves changing the DNA of an organism in the lab. Some people say it is dangerous and can upset the balance of nature. Other thinks it is a quick way to produce an organism with the most desirable traits. Why might people think it is dangerous? Give two examples. Then, tell how you feel about genetic engineering and why.

_____

_____

_____

_____

Fill in the circle next to the best answer.

4. Who is considered to the father of genetics?

(A) Gregor Mendel   (C) Jonas Salk

(B) Albert Einstein   (D) Alexander Fleming

Write *true* or *false*.

1. _____ Each organism in an ecosystem has an energy role.

2. _____ Consumers are organisms that can make their own food.

3. _____ Mushrooms are a type of decomposer.

4. _____ Herbivores and scavengers are types of producers.

How are carnivores and omnivores similar?

_____

_____

Write the name of the symbiotic relationship that exists between each pair of organisms. Then, explain the relationship.

1. flea and dog: _____

_____

2. mushroom and forest plant: _____

_____

3. remora fish and shark: _____

_____

Draw an example of an energy pyramid that can be found in a forest. Show at least four levels.

How does the level of energy change from one level of the pyramid to the next?

_____

_____

Explain the chemical process of photosynthesis and what it produces.

_____

_____

How are cellular respiration and photosynthesis alike in the carbon dioxide-oxygen cycle? How are they different?

_____

_____

_____

Day #1

Day #2

Day #3

Day #4

Assessment # 14

Fill in the circle next to the best answer.

1. Which of the following organisms are both decomposers?

   (A) rabbits and snakes

   (C) mushrooms and bacteria

   (B) vultures and giraffes

   (D) frogs and fungus

2. Which consumer feeds on the dead bodies of other animals?

   (A) herbivore

   (C) insectivore

   (B) scavenger

   (D) omnivore

Answer the questions.

3. Explain the difference between a food chain and a food web.

_____

_____

_____

4. Why are different types of symbiotic relationships important in an ecosystem? Select a symbiotic relationship and explain how it benefits an ecosystem.

_____

_____

_____

5. Explain two ways that competition can decrease the size of a rabbit population.

_____

_____

_____

Day #1

What is an adaptation?

_____

_____

Choose an animal. Tell two ways that it is adapted to its environment.

_____

_____

Day #2

Unscramble the letters in bold to make words that tell how organisms adapt.

1. Some animals have body shapes or colors they use as **floamacgue** to blend into their environment.
2. Some animals use **yimcrim**, so their bodies look like another dangerous organism.
3. The **mootcolnio** of an animal can help it move quickly to escape from a predator.
4. Some animals have bright body parts or loud voices that attract the **nettoniat** of members of its own kind.
5. Some animals have special body structures, like a turtle's hard shell, that give them **tropticone**.

Day #3

What is natural selection?

_____

_____

_____

_____

_____

Day #4

Why is there such a diversity of plant and animal life on Earth? Give three reasons.

_____

_____

_____

_____

_____

Assessment # 15

Assessment

Answer the questions.

1. How do variations develop? What affect do they have on a species?

_____

_____

_____

2. In the 1800s, the peppered moth had both light and dark wings. At first, there were many more light-winged moths than dark. The industrial revolution produced large amounts of dirt that darkened the trees. As a result, the population of dark-winged moths increased greatly, while the light-winged moths decreased to an all-time low. Write a paragraph that discusses the reasons for the population change, the adaptation that affected the population, and the role of natural selection in the process.

_____

_____

_____

_____

3. Several species, such as the dodo bird, are now extinct. Is the loss of a species harmful to diversity? Explain.

_____

_____

_____

Fill in the circle next to the best answer.

4. What kind of adaptations are the ears on a rabbit?

   (A) behavioral   (C) mutated

   (B) structural   (D) instinctive

Describe three ways that scientists classify plants.

_____

_____

_____

How is a dicot the same as and different from a monocot? Give an example of each.

_____

Write **P** in front of each substance that is important for growing a healthy plant.

_____ sun   _____ carbon dioxide

_____ water   _____ soil

_____ oxygen   _____ temperature

_____ fertilizer   _____ insects

Choose three substances from above. Tell how they make the plant healthy.

_____

Label the plant cell.

_____

_____

_____

How is a plant cell different from an animal cell? Why are these differences important?

_____

Use each word in a sentence to tell why it is important to plants.

photosynthesis _____

_____

autotroph _____

_____

eukaryote _____

_____

chlorophyll_____

_____

Assessment # 16

Fill in the circle next to the best answer.

1. What is the main source of energy for plants?

    (A) sugar   (C) decomposers

    (B) nutrients   (D) oxygen

2. Which is not a way to grow plants without seeds?

    (A) Roots are divided and replanted.

    (B) A leaf is replanted.

    (C) The stem of one plant is joined to an established root system.

    (D) A piece of a small plant is cut off and replanted.

Answer the questions.

3. What are three ways that plants interact with their non-living environment?

    _____

    _____

    _____

4. What is the nitrogen cycle? What parts do plants play in it?

    _____

    _____

    _____

    _____

5. Choose one plant. Tell three ways it is adapted to its environment.

    _____

    _____

Name

What are the three basic behaviors that animals exhibit?

_____

_____

_____

Why do animals exhibit these behaviors?

_____

_____

Explain the differences between learned behaviors and instinctive behaviors.

_____

_____

_____

Think about a time that you observed an animal. What instinctive behavior did the animal exhibit?

_____

Read each scenario. Write **conditioning**, **insight learning**, or **trial-and-error learning** to identify the behavior. Then, state another example of the behavior.

1. A woodpecker learns that pine trees provide the best worms.

_____

2. A cat comes running when she hears cat food being opened.

_____

3. A gorilla uses what he knows about opening locks to get a banana.

_____

What are two benefits that animals gain by migrating?

_____

_____

Do you think migration is a pattern of behavior? Explain.

_____

_____

_____

Assessment

Assessment # 17

Fill in the circle next to the best answer.

1. Mia gives her dog a treat each time he sits. What is Mia doing?

   (A) insight learning   (C) trial-and-error learning

   (B) migration   (D) conditioning

2. When butterflies travel from their summer homes in the United States to South America, what are they doing?

   (A) imprinting   (C) migrating

   (B) learning   (D) adapting

Answer the questions.

3. A turtle puts its head back in its shell when a larger animal approaches. Is this instinctive or learned behavior? Explain.

   _____

4. Charlie's dog jumps on guests when they come in the front door. Create a plan that Charlie can use to train his dog to sit when people come to visit.

   _____

   _____

   _____

5. Write a paragraph explaining how you have used insight learning to learn a new task.

   _____

   _____

   _____

   _____

   _____

Unscramble the letters in bold to make words that tell about stars.

1. The color of a star depends on its **furasce** temperature.
2. A star is created from a large cloud of dust and gas called a **ublane**.
3. When a star loses fuel and starts to die, it is called a **edr nitag**.
4. A **vpsuraneo** occurs when a dying star explodes.
5. The **tiweh fdarw** stage is usually the final stage in a star's life.
6. If a star's size decreases while its gravity increases, a **lkacb ohle** occurs.

What four characteristics do scientists use to classify stars?

_____

Write the name of the solar system body below each picture.

_____   _____   _____   _____

What is the difference in an asteroid and a meteoroid?

_____

Why is gravity so important to our solar system?

_____

_____

Explain why two objects fall to Earth at the same speed, regardless of size.

_____

_____

In 2006, the International Astronomical Association met to specifically define the word *planet*. As a result, Pluto, for many years the ninth planet, was characterized as a dwarf planet. What are the three characteristics scientists use to define a true planet?

_____

Why do you think scientists need definitions for the different types of planets?

_____

_____

Assessment # 18

Fill in the circle next to the best answer.

1. What color is the sun in the star spectrum?

   (A) purple   (C) red

   (B) yellow   (D) blue

2. Where is the asteroid belt located?

   (A) between Venus and Earth   (C) between Mars and Jupiter

   (B) between Jupiter and Saturn (D) between Mars and the sun

Answer the questions.

3. If objects falling to Earth fall at the same speed, why does it take so long for a feather to fall to the ground?

   _____

4. Why do you think astronomers made the decision to change Pluto's status? Do you agree or disagree? Explain.

   _____

   _____

   _____

   _____

5. Do you think it is important for human beings to explore space? Why or why not?

   _____

   _____

   _____

   _____

Name

Label the descriptions with **June solstice**, **December solstice**, **March/September equinox**.

1. Both of Earth's hemispheres receive the same amount of energy.
   _____

2. The south end of Earth's axis is tilted toward the sun. _____

3. The north end of Earth's axis is tilted toward the sun. _____

What would happen to temperatures if Earth's axis was not tilted?

_____

Write numbers **1** to **8** to show the correct order of the moon's phases.

_____ waxing crescent   _____ new moon

_____ full moon   _____ waxing gibbous

_____ waning gibbous   _____ waning crescent

_____ first quarter   _____ third quarter

What is an eclipse?

_____

Draw a picture to show a solar eclipse.

Explain how the moon's position affects the tides of Earth's oceans.

_____

_____

Does a new moon affect the tides differently than a quarter moon? Explain.

_____

_____

Assessment

Assessment # 19

Fill in the circle next to the best answer.

1. What causes seasons?

   Ⓐ Earth's orbit. Ⓒ the tilt of Earth's axis
   Ⓑ Earth's equator Ⓓ the phases of the moon

2. Which force causes the tides?

   Ⓐ gravity Ⓒ pressure
   Ⓑ momentum Ⓓ friction

3. When does a lunar eclipse take place?

   Ⓐ during a waxing gibbous moon Ⓒ during a waning crescent moon
   Ⓑ during a full moon Ⓓ during a new moon

Answer the questions.

4. Compare the moon's revolution around Earth with its rotation on its axis.

   _____

   _____

5. How many high tides occur each day? Explain.

   _____

   _____

   _____

6. The seasons have been studied and predicted for hundreds of years. Why do you think knowledge of the seasons was so important to early farmers?

   _____

   _____

   _____

What is the hydrosphere? List ten parts of the hydrosphere.

_____

_____

Why is the hydrosphere important? Identify three reasons.

_____

_____

Unscramble the words in bold to make words that tell about groundwater.

1. Rainwater falling to the ground and traveling through soil is called **fraltinotin**.
2. The zone of **tearnoia** is the area close to the surface of the soil where this occurs.
3. Further down, water **lrpoetcaes** through dirt and rocks.
4. The water finally ends up in the zone of **rustniaota**.
5. An **qfauire** holds a reserve of water inside rocks in the ground.

What is an estuary? Describe the type of plant and animal life that live in it.

_____

_____

_____

What makes a bog different from a swamp?

_____

_____

Seawater is also called _saltwater_. What two chemical elements found in seawater promote the use of this name?

_____

Describe what might happen to ocean wildlife when chemicals from a large ship are spilled into the ocean.

_____

_____

Assessment

Assessment # 20

Fill in the circle next to the best answer.

1. Chemically, what is the ocean?

   (A) a solid   (C) a suspension

   (B) a solution   (D) a base

2. Where is the greatest amount of freshwater found?

   (A) in clouds   (C) in rivers

   (B) underground   (D) in glaciers

3. Which of these is an example of flowing freshwater?

   (A) swamp   (C) lake

   (B) creek   (D) estuary

Answer the questions.

4. Why are clouds considered to be part of the hydrosphere?

   _____

   _____

5. Do you think that water is an inexhaustible resource? Explain.

   _____

   _____

6. Write a public service announcement explaining the importance of freshwater. Include three ways people can preserve its cleanliness.

   _____

   _____

   _____

   _____

What is atmosphere?

_____

_____

Write numbers **1** to **5** to show the order of the layers of Earth's atmosphere, starting with the layer closest to Earth

_____ mesosphere   _____ thermosphere

_____ stratosphere   _____ troposphere

_____ exosphere

Describe the troposphere. Use the words in the box in your description.

| dense | gravity | nitrogen | oxygen | water vapor | weather |

_____

_____

_____

_____

In which layer do shooting stars appear? What occurs in this layer to cause this phenomenon?

_____

_____

In which layer do most airplanes fly? Why don't they stay in the troposphere?

_____

_____

In which part of the atmosphere can the ozone layer be found? What does this layer do?

_____

_____

How is this kind of ozone different from the growing ozone in the troposphere?

_____

_____

Assessment

Assessment # 21

Fill in the circle next to the best answer.

1. In which layer do satellites most often orbit Earth?

    (A) troposphere   (C) thermosphere

    (B) mesosphere   (D) stratosphere

2. Which gas is the most common in the troposphere?

    (A) nitrogen   (C) helium

    (B) oxygen   (D) carbon dioxide

3. Which is the thinnest layer?

    (A) mesosphere   (C) exosphere

    (B) stratosphere   (D) troposphere

Answer the questions.

4. The ozone layer is often the topic of news reports. It has been reported that the ozone layer is slowly depleting. Why do you think so many people are interested in this element of the atmosphere? Cite two reasons in your discussion.

    _____

    _____

    _____

    _____

5. What do you think would happen to the atmosphere if there was no gravity? How could this affect life on Earth.

    _____

    _____

    _____

What is the difference between weather and climate?

_____

Describe the weather today.

_____

What is the climate in the place where you live?

_____

How can land affect climate? Give two examples.

_____

_____

How can water affect climate? Give two examples.

_____

_____

Write _true_ or _false_.

1. _____ Barometers measure the speed of wind.
2. _____ If you wanted to measure the humidity of an area, you would use a hygrometer.
3. _____ The home thermometer is the same thermometer climatologists use to measure the temperature of an area.
4. _____ A barometer is used to determine the air pressure in the atmosphere.
5. _____ Meteorologists use years of weather information to look for weather trends and patterns.

How is the climate in a rainforest in Brazil different from the climate in the Arizona desert?

_____

_____

What characteristics of these areas did you use to make this determination?

_____

_____

Assessment # 22

Assessment

Fill in the circle next to the best answer.

1. Which is not a factor in determining climate?

    (A) temperature   (C) humidity

    (B) trees   (D) wind

2. What is the weather phenomenon that is caused by changes in the speed of trade winds in the Pacific Ocean?

    (A) El Capitan   (C) Le Chien

    (B) El Niño   (D) Senorita

The chart below shows the average monthly temperatures and precipitation in Chicago, Illinois. Use the data to make a bar graph of the rainfall. Then, answer the questions.

Month	Temperature (°F)	Precipitation (in.)
Jan.	30	1.9
Feb.	34	1.6
Mar.	46	2.8
Apr.	59	3.8
May	71	3.2
June	81	4.1
July	84	4.0
Aug.	82	3.5
Sept.	75	3.1
Oct.	64	2.7
Nov.	49	2.9
Dec.	35	2.6

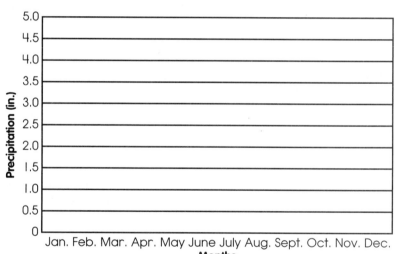

3. What is the climate of this Chicago? Explain how you know.

    _____

    _____

4. How does climate affect people? Name two ways.

    _____

    _____

Draw a line to match each word with its definition.

tectonic plates   the center of Earth

crust   the outer layer of Earth

mantle   a phenomenon created by the flowing metal in the planet

core   rock plates that float across the surface of Earth

solar winds   the layer made of molten rock, between Earth's core and crust

dynamo effect   a phenomenon that occurs when solar winds collide with the mesosphere

aurora borealis   a stream of charged particles ejected from the sun's atmosphere

What is the San Andreas Fault?

_____

_____

Describe what might happen to San Bernardino, since it is located on the San Andreas Fault.

_____

_____

Point Delgada
Point Arena
San Francisco
Hollister
Monterey
Parkfield
Simmler
Frazier Park
Santa Barbara
San Bernardino
Los Angeles
San Diego

What is the difference between a landslide and a mudflow?

_____

Suppose that you came across a slope that had been affected by creep. Write a description of what the trees and plants on this slope might look like.

_____

_____

_____

The Hawaiian Islands were formed by shield volcanoes. Mount Saint Helens is a composite volcano. What is the difference?

_____

List three ways volcanic eruptions impact Earth's surface.

_____

_____

_____

Assessment # 23

Fill in the circle next to the best answer.

1. How are a wildfire, a volcanic eruption, and a landslide alike?

    (A) They all burn.   (C) They are examples of erosion.

    (B) They are natural hazards.   (D) They were caused by glaciations.

2. What happens when two tectonic plates rub together?

    (A) erosion   (C) earthquake

    (B) sandstorm   (D) sinkhole

Answer the questions.

3. What effect does a river's slope have on a river's speed and sediment load?

    _____

    _____

4. Why do Earth's plates move? Describe the process.

    _____

    _____

    _____

    _____

    _____

5. Scientists constantly monitor plate movement and the activity of volcanoes.
    Why do they do this? Give two reasons.

    _____

    _____

    _____

Name

The National Aeronautics and Space Administration, or NASA, is the agency in the United States government that works to understand outer space. They send spacecraft and astronauts up to explore this last frontier.

What are three specific problems that people in space must deal with?

_____

_____

How are these problems solved?

_____

Day #1

NASA scientists look at specific problems and find ways to solve them. They develop materials and tools that keep the vehicles and people safe. Many of these materials are now a part of our daily lives. For example, astronauts needed to drill holes into the moon to get rock samples. The tool needed to have its own power source. A tool company invented cordless tools to solve the problem.

Why would a drill need to have its own power source in space?

_____

_____

Day #2

If you look up at the ceiling outside the bedrooms or kitchen, you will most likely see a smoke detector. Smoke detectors were first used on the Skylab Space Station in the 1970s. The space station was the first environment for astronauts to live in away from Earth.

Why is the smoke detector useful in our daily lives?

_____

_____

_____

Day #3

Food that is freeze-dried has no moisture. As a result, it is very lightweight, stores compactly, and does not need refrigeration. Moreover, freeze-dried food can last for years. It was another NASA invention. Today, these packets of food are popular with hikers and campers.

Why was freeze-dried food important for space travel?

_____

What are two examples of freeze-dried food that you use?

_____

Day #4

Assessment

Assessment # 24

Read the paragraph. Then, answer the questions.

Racecar drivers use two inventions that were first developed for astronauts. The suits they wear have a special coating that is less likely to burn. However, these suits can also trap the body's heat, making the suit very hot to wear. So racecar drivers also use another NASA technology called *cool suits*. A special garment is worn next to the body under the suit. Chilled liquid is pumped throughout the garment.

1. What problems did each kind of clothing solve for astronauts?

_____

_____

2. Why would the suits with a special coating that did not burn be good for a racecar driver?

_____

_____

3. How do you think a cool suit rids the body of heat?

_____

_____

4. How else might a cool suit be used?

_____

_____

5. How does communication between scientists affect society?

_____

_____

Optical microscopes rely on lenses, mirrors, and radiant light to view things out eyes can't see. The first microscope was actually made when Hans and Zacharias Janssen, glass grinders, placed two lenses in a tube. However, Anton van Leeuwenhoek is credited with inventing the first microscope. Unlike other scientists of his day, he did not go to school or speak multiple languages. He was curious about the world and persistent in finding answers. In all, he made almost 500 different versions of the microscope. Van Leeuwenhoek was able to view blood, insects, and bacteria with a single lens.

Was van Leeuwenhoek a good scientist? Explain.

_____

Label the microscope.

Use the labels above to complete the sentences.
1. A lens in the _____ helps make the image on the slide bigger.
2. The slide sets on the _____.
3. The _____ illuminates the image on the slide.
4. The _____ brings the image into view, and adjusting the _____ makes the image sharper.
5. By rotating the _____, the magnification increases, making the image larger.
6. To move a microscope, one hand holds the curved _____, and one hand is placed under the base.

Write numbers **1** through **7** to show the steps needed to set up a microscope.

_____ Look through the eyepiece using the 4X objective.

_____ Repeat the process using 40X objective.

_____ Adjust the course focus.

_____ Put the slide on the microscope.

_____ Repeat the process using 10X objective.

_____ Adjust the fine focus.

_____ Turn on the light.

Name

Assessment # 25

Read the paragraph. Then, answer the questions.

You use an optical microscope in the lab. This kind of microscope uses light and lenses to magnify objects that cannot be seen by the naked eye. The strongest ones can enlarge images up to 1,000 times their original size. But many things in our world are much smaller. An electron microscope increases an image up to two million times. Instead of bouncing light, the electron microscope shoots a thin beam of electrons back and forth across the surface of an object that has been freeze-dried and sealed in a vacuum. The microscope reads the electrons and produces a 3-D image of the object on a computer monitor.

1. How is an optical microscope the same as and different from an electron microscope?

   _____

2. Why does an object need to be sealed in a vacuum before being viewed by an electron microscope?

   _____

3. Why are microscopes important tools?

   _____

Fill in the circle next to the best answer.

4. How do you find magnification?

   (A) Multiply the eyepiece times the objective.

   (B) Divide the objective by the eyepiece.

   (C) Divide the numbers of the course and fine focus.

   (D) Multiple the objective times the fine focus.

5. What material is most often used to prepare a slide?

   (A) iodine   (C) hydrochloride

   (B) saline solution   (D) bleach

Forensic scientists are people who use science to solve crimes. They look at evidence, like fingerprints, skeletal remains, hair, and soil, to get clues. Choose and describe three process skills a forensic scientist would use.

_____

_____

What do you think would be the most interesting part of being a forensic scientist?

_____

Day #1

Draw a line to match the name of each fingerprint pattern with its picture.

loop   arch   whorl

What type of fingerprints do you have? How are they the same as and different from the pattern above? Give two specific examples of each.

_____

_____

Day #2

Trace evidence are very small pieces of material left at a crime scene that may not be seen with the naked eye. This kind of evidence includes hair, clothes fibers, blood, and skin cells.

What are two tools that a forensics scientist would need to study trace evidence? Explain their use.

_____

What three characteristics could a scientist use to identify hair samples?

_____

Day #3

Unscramble the letters in bold to make words that tell about DNA.

1. Only **taidcline sniwt** have the same DNA.
2. DNA is a long spiral chain of **dtuelconsie**.
3. Two long chains that twist around each other create a shape called a **lebudo-lehix**.
4. A **sochromoem** is a tightly wound group of DNA cells.
5. DNA is the **nstirutnoic** manual for organisms.

What two methods might a forensic scientist use to collect a DNA sample?

_____

Day #4

Assessment

Assessment # 26

Fill in the circle next to the best answer.

1. Which is not a type of fingerprint?

   Ⓐ swirl   Ⓒ arch

   Ⓑ loop   Ⓓ accidental

2. What tool might a forensic scientist use to find hair, fibers, or blood on a surface or object?

   Ⓐ ink prints   Ⓒ Luma Light

   Ⓑ dental cement   Ⓓ criminal files

Answer the questions.

3. Name three clues forensic scientists might use to determine the author of a written document at a crime scene?

   _____

   _____

4. What are two specific pieces of evidence that would convict a criminal? Why?

   _____

   _____

5. How would knowing about the life cycle and characteristics of decomposers help a forensic scientist?

   _____

   _____

6. Do you think that a forensic scientist uses the scientific method to solve crimes? Explain.

   _____

Draw a line to match each field of science with its definition.

audiologist	works with Earth's atmosphere and everything in it
gemologist	works with the design, construction, and testing of aircraft
physiologist	identifies, grades, and evaluates precious stones and minerals
pharmacist	prepares and dispenses medicines
horticulturist	diagnoses and treats hearing loss and imbalance problems
meteorologist	studies the chemical, mechanical, and physical make-up of organisms
aeronautics engineer	cultivates fruits, vegetables, flowers, or ornamental plants

Day #1

Look at each career. Identify a science concept that a person in this field needs to know to do the job.

architect _____

detective _____

artist _____

surveyor _____

pilot _____

science fiction writer _____

Day #2

Look at each school subject. List two science careers that people can do if this is their area of interest.

math _____

language arts _____

health _____

physical education _____

art _____

Day #3

The world is constantly changing. Does science impact these changes? Give at least two examples in your discussion.

_____

_____

_____

_____

_____

Day #4

Assessment # 27

Assessment

Answer the questions.

1. What career would you like to have? Describe the job and explain three ways that you would use science in it.

_____

_____

_____

_____

2. Choose a sport. Explain three ways that science impacts it. Think about the skills needed in the sport, people who support the sport, or basic science principles related to it.

_____

_____

_____

_____

_____

3. Is it important for you to take science now and throughout your school career? Explain your opinion. Support it with at least two examples.

_____

_____

_____

_____

Week #28: Computer Use

Use each word in a sentence that tells its function on a computer.

hardware:_____

_____

software: _____

_____

document:_____

_____

format: _____

_____

What are three reasons you use the Internet?

_____

_____

What are two benefits of e-mail?

_____

_____

Complete each sentence to tell about a computer safety rule.

1. Never give out your personal information, such as _____.
2. You should not agree to meet people _____.
3. You create passwords to protect your privacy, so you should not _____.
4. Make sure to protect your computer by using _____.
5. If you see something on the computer or are involved in a conversation that makes you feel uncomfortable, _____.
6. Before downloading songs, programs, or other materials, _____.

Identify four computer programs and tell how you use them.

_____

_____

_____

_____

_____

Assessment

Assessment # 28

Answer the questions.

1. Imagine that you are "chatting" online with a friend. Write a brief message telling about something that recently happened. Use the same language that you would type on the computer.

_____

_____

2. Now imagine that you are "chatting" online with an older family member. Would you use the same abbreviations, language, and words? Why or why not?

_____

_____

3. Why is it important to think about your audience before typing messages?

_____

_____

4. What are two positive and two negative aspects of computers in our society?

_____

_____

5. Think about all the places that use computers, including school, stores, transportation, and home. How do computers impact your daily life?

_____

_____

_____

Write one function of each system.

1. skeletal system _____
2. digestive system _____
3. muscular system _____
4. endocrine system _____
5. integumentary system _____
6. reproductive system _____
7. nervous system _____
8. excretory system _____

Name the three types of muscle. Give an example of each.

_____

_____

Name the three functions of the digestive system?

_____

_____

Write a word to complete each sentence to tell about the respiratory system.
1. The _____ are the main organs in the respiratory system.
2. The _____ is a muscle that helps pull in and push out air.
3. Tiny hairs in the nose, called _____, filter out dangerous particles, like dust and pollen.
4. Small capillaries in your _____ warm the air as it enters.
5. The warmed air travels down the _____ in your neck.
6. This tube breaks into two tubes, each called the _____.
7. The tubes keep dividing into smaller parts and end in tiny air sacs, called _____.
8. Capillaries in the circulatory system surround the sacs and exchange the carbon dioxide for clean _____ in the red blood cells.

What are the two parts of the nervous system? What does each part control?

_____

_____

What is a reflex? Give an example of a reflex.

_____

_____

Assessment

Assessment # 29

Fill in the circle next to the best answer.

1. Which is not part of the respiratory system?

   (A) lungs   (C) alveoli

   (B) bladder   (D) nose

2. Why is the backbone a flexible structure?

   (A) It is made of solid cartilage.

   (B) The 26 vertebrae allow it to bend and flex.

   (C) The bones in this body part are softer than other body parts.

   (D) The bones in this body part are not connected.

3. Which internal organ do your ribs protect?

   (A) brain   (C) heart

   (B) bladder   (D) liver

Answer the questions.

4. Explain what occurs in the muscular system when the arm is bent and straightened.

   _____

   _____

5. Label the skeleton.

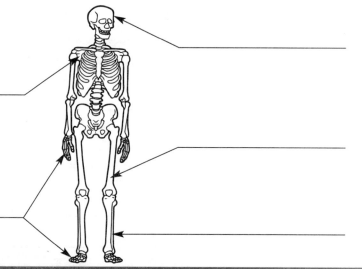

Some scientists have identified six basic emotions. Write **E** in front of the words that name these emotions.

_____ love	_____ fear	_____ loneliness
_____ surprise	_____ sadness	_____ happiness
_____ eagerness	_____ hunger	_____ thirst
_____ tiredness	_____ disgust	_____ anger

Choose two of the basic emotions. Identify a situation that makes you experience each feeling.

_____

Day #1

Write a word to complete each sentence to tell about emotions.

1. Emotions are reactions in the _____ system.
2. The _____ is the main organ that controls emotions.
3. There are 42 _____ in the face that shape it to show emotions.
4. The body position, physical movements, and tone of _____ also show how a person is feeling.
5. Dopamine is a chemical the body releases when someone feels _____.
6. The same part of the brain that produces anger also produces _____.

Day #2

What are two ways that emotions affect behavior? Give an example of each.

_____

_____

_____

Why is fear a good emotion to have?

_____

_____

Day #3

Phineas Gage worked for a railroad company in 1848. An explosion sent a thin iron rod sailing through the air. The rod entered his left cheekbone and exited through the top of his skull, damaging the left side of his brain. Gage survived and continued to talk and walk immediately afterwards. However, his personality suffered. Before the accident, Gage was responsible, sociable, and made good decisions. After the accident, Gage was impatient and impulsive. He was incapable of making good decisions.

What can you conclude from this account?

_____

Day #4

Assessment

Assessment # 30

Answer the questions.

1. Do you think people can fake emotions? Explain.

_____

_____

2. Can emotions affect the health of your body? Explain.

_____

_____

3. Extreme emotions can happen when a person is not physically or mentally healthy. For example, depression is the extreme emotion of sadness. How might drug and alcohol abuse be the result of the extreme happiness?

_____

_____

4. Darria has a friend who has been acting differently. She has not been eating as much and is avoiding her friends. What should Darria do?

_____

_____

Fill in the circle next the best answer.

5. What happens to the body when a person feels fear?

  (A) The heart beats faster.   (C) The body gets sleepy.

  (B) The arm muscles relax.   (D) The body temperature increases.

6. Which is not a process of the brain in response to an emotion?

  (A) react   (C) recognize

  (B) show   (D) ignore

Write *true* or *false*.

1. _____ Runners need more carbohydrates in their diets than people who do not exercise.
2. _____ You can survive longer without food than water.
3. _____ There are seven nutrients needed by the body.
4. _____ The higher the number of calories in a food, the more energy it provides.
5. _____ The more active you are, the less energy you need.

Write a word to correctly complete each sentence.

1. Cardiovascular health deals with keeping the _____ in good working order.
2. One way to maintain a healthy heart is to get physical _____ several times each week.
3. You should also _____ diet that is low in fat, sodium, and cholesterol.
4. Be sure to give your body at least seven hours of _____ each night.
5. Avoid alcohol and _____ that will change the body's chemistry.
6. Finally, talk with a friend or an adult if you are having feelings of _____, because it can create trouble for your cardiovascular system when you are older.

What is hygiene?

_____

_____

What are three good hygiene practices you follow?

_____

_____

_____

What are three safety precautions you should follow when you are out in the sun? Explain why.

_____

_____

_____

_____

_____

Assessment

Assessment # 31

Fill in the circle next to the best answer.

1. Which of these foods is heart healthy?

   (A) soda   (C) orange

   (B) butter   (D) potato chips

2. According to the Food Guide Pyramid, from which group should you eat the least servings?

   (A) fats, oils, and sweets   (C) bread, cereal, rice, and pasta

   (B) milk, yogurt, and cheese   (D) vegetables

Answer the questions.

3. What are the six nutrients your body needs to grow and stay healthy? Explain what each does and an example of each.

   _____

   _____

   _____

   _____

   _____

   _____

4. What are three things you do to maintain a healthy lifestyle? What are three things you could change to improve your health?

   _____

   _____

   _____

   _____

List four reasons people take prescription drugs.

_____

_____

Is it possible to take too many prescription drugs? Explain.

_____

_____

Day #1

Write *true* or *false*.

1. _____ Long-term alcohol abuse might result in liver dysfunction.
2. _____ Alcohol affects every body system.
3. _____ Alcohol might impair judgment. For example, driving a car might be more difficult.
4. _____ Alcohol improves your motor skills.
5. _____ Alcohol is considered a stimulant.
6. _____ Alcoholism is a disease.
7. _____ The lower the blood alcohol content, the more drunk a person is.

Day #2

What is an anabolic steroid?

_____

List three negative effects of anabolic steroids on the body.

_____

_____

_____

Day #3

What are three ways that smoking affects the body?

_____

What are two reasons that people start smoking?

_____

Can breathing cigarette smoke for a long time cause problems for a non-smoker? Explain.

_____

Day #4

Assessment # 32

Fill in the circle next to the best answer.

1. Which is a not an effect of alcohol?

   (A) blurred vision

   (B) impaired ability to make decisions

   (C) improved muscle coordination

   (D) changes in mood

2. Which is not an effect of inhalants?

   (A) sleepiness

   (B) headaches

   (C) difficulty breathing

   (D) nervousness

3. Imagine that a friend has told you that she is thinking about taking diet pills to increase her energy level and to lose some weight. You know that the pills she is describing are really amphetamines. What will you tell your friend? Write a paragraph arguing against the use of these pills. Use what you know about drugs and the importance of a healthy lifestyle to persuade her to stay away from diet pills.

   _____

   _____

   _____

   _____

4. Explain the effect that stimulants have on the nervous system.

   _____

   _____

5. Why do you think over-the-counter drugs and prescription drugs are sold in a pharmacy?

   _____

   _____

   _____

What is a pathogen?

_____

What are the four types of human pathogens? Give an example of a disease caused by each.

_____

_____

_____

_____

Describe the four main ways diseases spread.

_____

_____

_____

What are three ways to prevent the spread of diseases?

_____

_____

Explain how your skin acts as a barrier to infection.

_____

_____

What are three other ways that your body fights infections?

_____

_____

_____

Write **C** if the disease is communicable. Write **N** if it is noncommunicable.

1. diabetes   _____
2. chicken pox   _____
3. strep throat   _____
4. cancer   _____
5. pink eye   _____

Explain one similarity and one difference between communicable and noncommunicable diseases.

_____

Assessment

Assessment # 33

Fill in the circle next to the best answer.

1. Which of these is a communicable disease?

    (A) leukemia   (C) allergies

    (B) hepatitis   (D) arthritis

2. Which of these is not a barrier to disease?

    (A) skin   (C) toenails

    (B) mouth   (D) stomach

3. What causes lyme disease?

    (A) tick bites   (C) allergies

    (B) mosquito bites   (D) cancer

Answer the questions.

4. Some people believe that you can catch a cold from playing outside in the cold weather. Is it possible? Explain.

    _____

    _____

    _____

    _____

5. Can the body develop and immunity to disease? Explain.

    _____

    _____

    _____

    _____

    _____

Look at the chart. Make a graph to show the data.

Kind of Trash	Percentage (%)
paper	40
yard trimmings	18
metals	8
plastics	8
food scraps	7
glass	7
other	12

Why did you choose the graph you did?

_____

What three conclusions can you make from the data presented in the chart?

_____

_____

_____

_____

_____

_____

What are the three R's for helping the environment? Write a sentence using each and tell how you practice it.

_____

_____

_____

_____

_____

What is a mulch pile? How is it part of the carbon dioxide–oxygen cycle?

_____

_____

_____

List three ways to reuse a paper towel tube.

_____

_____

Assessment

Assessment # 34

Answer the questions.

1. What are the four parts of Earth's system? How can recycling impact each part?

_____

_____

_____

_____

_____

2. Eco-fashion is a growing trend where old clothes and plastic products are sewn together to create one-of-a-kind, high-end fashion pieces. Think of several items of clothing that you have outgrown or do not like anymore. Find a way to craft them into a new, stunning piece of clothing. Think of a way to add plastic. Draw a picture of the clothing in the box. Then, write a description of the pieces you used in your drawing.

_____

_____

_____

Draw a line to match each scientist with his or her scientific achievement.

Marie Curie — author of the theory of relativity

Albert Einstein — discovered the benefits of radium and radioactive therapies

Isaac Newton — anthropologist who studied women's roles in various societies

Lewis Howard Latimer — inventor, draftsman, and engineer instrumental in improving lighting

Margaret Mead — author of the three laws of motion

Isaac Newton is one of the most famous scientists in history. His first experiments dealt with bending light using a prism. After much experimentation, Newton discovered that white light could be separated into colors as it moved through a prism. Newton stated that light consisted of streams of very small particles. He shared his ideas in a journal, but they were not accepted because other scientists were unable to duplicate his experiments.

How might failures and lack of acceptance by peers encourage a scientist?

_____

_____

Lewis Latimer received a patent for inventing the screw bottom in a bulb. What problem did he most likely solve?

_____

_____

Latimer was a very talented draftsman. He made careful drawings and diagrams of all his ideas. How would this be helpful in the scientific community?

_____

_____

Margaret Mead studied primitive cultures. Define the word *primitive* in this context.

_____

_____

Name two primitive cultures that you would be interested in studying and why.

_____

_____

Assessment

Assessment # 35

Answer the questions.

1. Consider the world events taking place during the 1940s. Why do you think Albert Einstein might have moved to the United States to continue his studies and experiments?

    _____

    _____

2. Lewis Howard Latimer drafted many patents for inventions still used today. Why do you think it is important for inventors to patent their inventions?

    _____

    _____

3. Read the quote from Margaret Mead below. Explain it using your own words.

    "Anthropology demands the open-mindedness with which one must look and listen, record in astonishment and wonder that which one would not have been able to guess."

    _____

    _____

4. Marie Curie died from radiation poisoning due to her experiments with radium. How has experimentation changed so that scientists better protect themselves and safe guard the health of those they are working with? Cite two changes.

    _____

    _____

    _____

    _____

Human beings are the smartest animals on Earth. They can solve problems, communicate, and use tools. They also recognize their image in a mirror, and they show emotions. Using these criteria, scientists have been studying other animal species to see if they might be considered intelligent. The results are quite surprising!

Why would recognizing a self-image in a mirror be a sign of intelligence?

_____

_____

Day #1

Rocky is a sea lion that understands sign language. Her trainers taught her hand signals that stand for colors, objects, and actions. A trainer can put several objects in the pool with Rocky and make two signals telling Rocky what to do. For example, the trainer can make a signal for "ball" and another for "tail touch." Rocky would understand the message and swim down and touch the ball with her tail.

Do you think that a sea lion is an intelligent animal? Why or why not?

_____

_____

Day #2

Some parrots can be trained to talk. They say words, sounds of appliances, and whistle. Irene Pepperberg has been working with a parrot named *Alex* for many years. Not only does Alex talk, but he can tell the color, shape, and material of an object that Pepperberg holds up. He can even count and understand abstract concepts, like different and same. Now, that's a smart bird!

Do you think that a parrot is an intelligent animal? Why or why not?

_____

_____

Day #3

Elephants are the biggest land animals. Scientists have been observing them to see just how smart they are. One characteristic to decide if an animal is intelligent is if it uses tools. An elephant will pick up sticks to scratch their backs, throw logs into trees to weight the branches down to get leaves, and smash things with rocks.

Do you think that an elephant is an intelligent animal? Why or why not?

_____

_____

_____

Day #4

Assessment # 36

Read the paragraph. Then, answer the questions.

Chimpanzees are the closest relatives to human beings because of their chemical make-up and physical structure. Increased research shows they also exhibit many characteristics of intelligence. They are very social animals that live in large groups. Jane Goodall, a naturalist, spent many years in Africa studying the animals in the wild. Goodall observed that the chimps used their voices, faces, and hands to tell others how they felt. They fished ants out of the ground with blades of grass and opened nuts with rocks. Amazingly, they fought other troops of monkeys, swinging sticks as clubs to kill each other. Moreover, Goodall saw their emotions. One chimp was so upset about the death of his mother that he stopped eating and died, too.

1. According to the article, what are three ways that scientists judge the intelligence of chimps? Explain.

_____

_____

2. Why is it important to learn about animals? How does the information help us learn more about human beings?

_____

_____

3. What three process skills can a scientist use when working with animals? Explain their use.

_____

_____

4. Some animal rights groups believe that is unethical to experiment and work with animals. Why? What is your opinion?

_____

_____

Write *true* or *false*.

1. _____ Recycled tires are used in playground materials.
2. _____ All pesticides are harmless to pets and human beings.
3. _____ Some tuna nets still collect dolphins and tortoises.
4. _____ Most plastic shopping bags are biodegradable.
5. _____ Scientists are studying the possibility of using ocean waves as energy resources.
6. _____ Changes that people make on Earth cannot result in the extinction of animals.
7. _____ A wildlife refuge is a place where animals are protected.

Day #1

Look at each appliance. Identify an energy-saving alternative.

dryer _____

automobile _____

television _____

vacuum _____

electric mixer _____

electric blanket _____

Day #2

Explain how an increase in human population impacts other species on Earth.

_____

_____

Do you think that the extinction of one species of animal or insect may impact your life? Explain.

_____

_____

Day #3

Give one example of a personal or local environmental issue and one example of a national or global issue. What is your opinion on these two topics?

_____

_____

_____

_____

Day #4

Assessment # 37

Answer the questions.

1. What are three ways to prevent overfishing?

_____

_____

_____

2. Look at the energyguide label. What information does it give? How does it help a consumer shop for appliances?

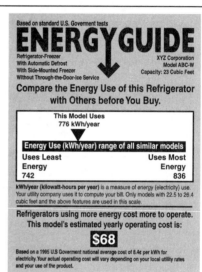

_____

_____

_____

_____

3. Would the appliance above be a good purchase? Why or why not?

_____

_____

4. Explain the difference between clear-cutting and selective cutting.

_____

_____

Fill in the circle next to the best answer.

5. Which item is often recycled?

(A) paper

(B) steel

(C) glass

(D) all of the above

Name

In A.D. 79, Mount Vesuvius erupted violently and sent ash and lava raining down on the city of Pompeii. Lava also flowed out of the vent and into the city. Archaeologists found the perfect remains of people, houses, and other artifacts. Why was the town so well preserved?

_____

Name two forensic clues that archaeologists might have used to determine what happened during the eruption.

_____

Day #1

There are many huge stone statues on Easter Island. However, there are no trees and no people. Archeologists believe that the inhabitants became obsessed with their statues. Because the statues were so large, they cut eventually cut down all the trees to help move them. How could the loss of trees lead to the loss of a total population?

_____

_____

_____

Day #2

Archaeologists have theorized that the inhabitants of Tiahuanaco abandoned life in the Lake Titicaca region because of a severe drought. Do you think something similar to this might happen if an extended, severe drought occurred in this country? Explain.

_____

_____

_____

Day #3

Some scientists believe that an advanced civilization lived on a continent called _Atlantis._ A cataclysmic event caused it to sink into the ocean. A written account from a respected ancient Greek, Plato, mentions its existence. However, no evidence has been found to either prove or disprove the theory. Could Atlantis exist? Support your opinion using two scientific facts.

_____

_____

_____

Day #4

Assessment

Assessment # 38

Answer the questions.

1. Why do scientists study lost populations? Give three reasons.

_____

_____

_____

2. Some of the information about lost civilizations has been passed down through myths and stories. How might scientists use the information?

_____

_____

_____

3. The people of Easter Island used all the trees. How has the use of trees changed to prevent this resource from disappearing in the world today?

_____

_____

_____

Fill in the circle next to the best answer.

4. Which of these is not considered a lost civilization?

(A) Tiahuanaco   (C) Pompeii

(B) Atlantis   (D) Halloween Island

5. Which scientist works most often with ancient sites?

(A) archeologist   (C) conservationist

(B) meteorologist   (D) microbiologist

Money has its roots in ancient China. At first, the people used cowrie shells for money. Later, they melted copper to make coins. Once the Chinese invented paper, they used it to make print money.

Why do you think the Chinese began to use coins instead of shells as their form of money?

_____

_____

_____

Some people try to make fake dollar bills in a process known as *counterfeiting*. Many governments take steps to prevent this activity by using a special printing process. In intaglio printing, the images are made with fine lines to create intricate details. When photocopied, these lines become blurred.

Why would photocopying a fine line make it look blurred?

_____

_____

_____

The words in the box name security features on bills. Write the name of the security feature next to its definition.

watermark	color-shifting ink	security thread

_____—by tilting the note up and down, the ink goes through a series of color changes.

_____—a faint image inside paper that can be seen from either side.

_____—a plastic strip running through a note that turns yellow when placed under ultraviolet light.

List two ways money can be exchanged without the use of paper bills or coins.

_____

_____

List two reasons why people might prefer using digital money to actual bills or coins.

_____

_____

Assessment # 39

Fill in the circle next to the best answer.

1. Which shells were used as currency in ancient China?

   (A) clam shells   (C) conch shells

   (B) cowrie shells   (D) starfish

2. What is the main material used in currency paper?

   (A) cotton   (C) polyester

   (B) silk   (D) spandex

Answer the questions.

3. Current U.S. bills must be made to withstand the wear and tear of circulation. List three ways paper bills may be damaged in the circulation process.

   _____

   _____

   _____

4. List two reasons people may be hesitant to use digital money rather than paper bills, coins, or checks.

   _____

   _____

5. People are increasingly using their computer for home banking and shopping. Do you think that coins and bills will become unnecessary in the future? Explain.

   _____

   _____

   _____

Week #40: Native Americans and Their Resources

The teepee was a common shelter for many Native-American tribes. What resources were needed to make it?

_____

_____

Why was there a hole near the top of the teepee?

_____

_____

Early Anasazi Indians built their houses, or pueblos, in the sides of canyon walls. Why was this a good location?

_____

_____

What resources were used to build these structures?

_____

_____

Paintings have been found on the walls of many Native-American dwellings. How do these paintings help anthropologists learn about the Indians' cultures?

_____

_____

What resources were used to paint these images?

_____

_____

When moving, some Native Americans used a travois, a kind of sled, made by crossing two poles into a "V" shape. The crossed part was tied to the animal, and the other ends dragged on the ground. How did this system make it easier to travel? Describe two ways.

_____

_____

_____

_____

Assessment # 40

Assessment

Fill in the circle next to the best answer.

1. Which was not used for making dyes?

    (A) berries   (C) ash

    (B) blood   (D) wool

2. Which crops were grown by most Native-American tribes?

    (A) squash and corn   (C) soybeans and basil

    (B) watermelon and tomatoes (D) sunflowers and parsley

Answer the questions.

3. Name two uses for bone in Native-American society.

    _____

    _____

4. Look at each buffalo part. Tell how the Native Americans may have used each.

    horn: _____

    hooves: _____

    tongue: _____

    hide: _____

    hair: _____

    muscles: _____

    feces: _____

5. It is a well-known fact that the Indian befriended the Pilgrims and taught them to plant fish with their seeds. Why?

    _____

Answer Key

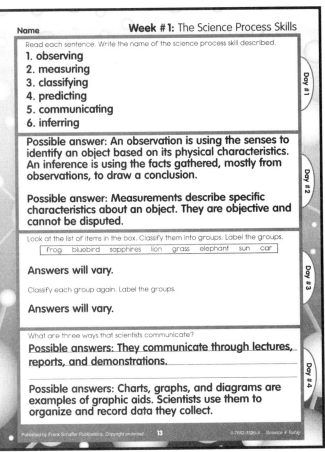

Name

Week #1: The Science Process Skills

Read each sentence. Write the name of the science process skill described.

1. observing
2. measuring
3. classifying
4. predicting
5. communicating
6. inferring

Day #1

Possible answer: An observation is using the senses to identify an object based on its physical characteristics. An inference is using the facts gathered, mostly from observations, to draw a conclusion.

Possible answer: Measurements describe specific characteristics about an object. They are objective and cannot be disputed.

Day #2

Look at the list of items in the box. Classify them into groups. Label the groups.

| frog | bluebird | sapphires | lion | grass | elephant | sun | car |

Answers will vary.

Classify each group again. Label the groups.

Answers will vary.

Day #3

What are three ways that scientists communicate?

Possible answers: They communicate through lectures, reports, and demonstrations.

Possible answers: Charts, graphs, and diagrams are examples of graphic aids. Scientists use them to organize and record data they collect.

Day #4

Published by Frank Schaffer Publications. Copyright protected. 13   0-7682-3526-X *Science 4 Today*

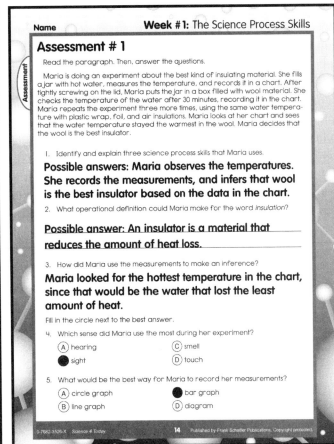

Name

Week #1: The Science Process Skills

Assessment

Assessment # 1

Read the paragraph. Then, answer the questions.

Maria is doing an experiment about the best kind of insulating material. She fills a jar with hot water, measures the temperature, and records it in a chart. After tightly screwing on the lid, Maria puts the jar in a box filled with wool material. She checks the temperature of the water after 30 minutes, recording it in the chart. Maria repeats the experiment three more times, using the same water temperature with plastic wrap, foil, and air insulations. Maria looks at her chart and sees that the water temperature stayed the warmest in the wool. Maria decides that the wool is the best insulator.

1. Identify and explain three science process skills that Maria uses.

Possible answers: Maria observes the temperatures. She records the measurements, and infers that wool is the best insulator based on the data in the chart.

2. What operational definition could Maria make for the word *insulation*?

Possible answer: An insulator is a material that reduces the amount of heat loss.

3. How did Maria use the measurements to make an inference?

Maria looked for the hottest temperature in the chart, since that would be the water that lost the least amount of heat.

Fill in the circle next to the best answer.

4. Which sense did Maria use the most during her experiment?
   - (A) hearing
   - ● sight
   - (C) smell
   - (D) touch

5. What would be the best way for Maria to record her measurements?
   - (A) circle graph
   - (B) line graph
   - ● bar graph
   - (D) diagram

0-7682-3526-X *Science 4 Today*   14   Published by Frank Schaffer Publications. Copyright protected.

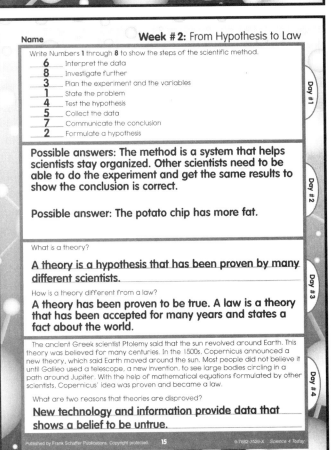

Name

Week #2: From Hypothesis to Law

Write Numbers **1** through **8** to show the steps of the scientific method.

- **6** Interpret the data
- **8** Investigate further
- **3** Plan the experiment and the variables
- **1** State the problem
- **4** Test the hypothesis
- **5** Collect the data
- **7** Communicate the conclusion
- **2** Formulate a hypothesis

Day #1

Possible answers: The method is a system that helps scientists stay organized. Other scientists need to be able to do the experiment and get the same results to show the conclusion is correct.

Possible answer: The potato chip has more fat.

Day #2

What is a theory?

A theory is a hypothesis that has been proven by many different scientists.

Day #3

How is a theory different from a law?
A theory has been proven to be true. A law is a theory that has been accepted for many years and states a fact about the world.

The ancient Greek scientist Ptolemy said that the sun revolved around Earth. This theory was believed for many centuries. In the 1500s, Copernicus announced a new theory, which said Earth moved around the sun. Most people did not believe it until Galileo used a telescope, a new invention, to see large bodies circling in a path around Jupiter. With the help of mathematical equations formulated by other scientists, Copernicus' idea was proven and became a law.

What are two reasons that theories are disproved?
New technology and information provide data that shows a belief to be untrue.

Day #4

Published by Frank Schaffer Publications. Copyright protected. 15   0-7682-3526-X *Science 4 Today*

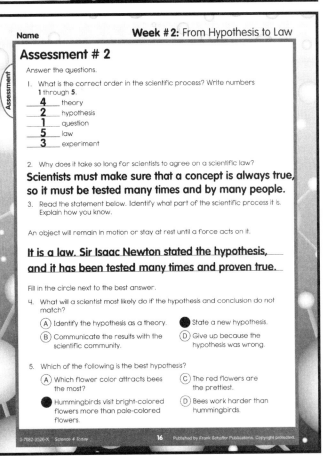

Name

Week #2: From Hypothesis to Law

Assessment

Assessment # 2

Answer the questions.

1. What is the correct order in the scientific process? Write numbers **1** through **5**.
   - **4** theory
   - **2** hypothesis
   - **1** question
   - **5** law
   - **3** experiment

2. Why does it take so long for scientists to agree on a scientific law?

Scientists must make sure that a concept is always true, so it must be tested many times and by many people.

3. Read the statement below. Identify what part of the scientific process it is. Explain how you know.

An object will remain in motion or stay at rest until a force acts on it.

It is a law. Sir Isaac Newton stated the hypothesis, and it has been tested many times and proven true.

Fill in the circle next to the best answer.

4. What will a scientist most likely do if the hypothesis and conclusion do not match?
   - (A) Identify the hypothesis as a theory.
   - (B) Communicate the results with the scientific community.
   - ● State a new hypothesis.
   - (D) Give up because the hypothesis was wrong.

5. Which of the following is the best hypothesis?
   - (A) Which flower color attracts bees the most?
   - ● Hummingbirds visit bright-colored flowers more than pale-colored flowers.
   - (C) The red flowers are the prettiest.
   - (D) Bees work harder than hummingbirds.

0-7682-3526-X *Science 4 Today*   16   Published by Frank Schaffer Publications. Copyright protected.

Answer Key

Possible answers:

Characteristic	Standard Units	Metric Units
Mass	pound	gram
Liquid Capacity	quart	liter
Length	inch	centimeter
Distance	mile	kilometer
Temperature	Fahrenheit	Celsius

What measurement system is used in the science community?

The metric system is used in the science community.

Why do all scientists use this system?

Possible answer: The metric system allows scientists all around the world to understand the data gathered, even if they do not speak the same language.

Possible answers: They both have a scale and category names. The bar graph shows the total amount in each category, while the line graph focuses on how one characteristic changes over time.

A nutritionist would use a circle graph. A circle graph shows percentages in a whole.

List five important tools commonly used by scientists in all fields and explain their uses.

Answers will vary.

Day #1 · Day #2 · Day #3 · Day #4

Assessment # 3

Complete the page.

1. Choose a device, such as a computer, cell phone, or television. Draw and label a diagram to show its parts.

Answers will vary.

2. Laura helped a park ranger count the number of trees in an acre. She recorded it in the chart below. Draw a graph to show the data.

Trees	Number
Pine	28
Oak	11
Maple	3

Answers will vary.

3. Explain why you chose the kind of graph above.

Answers will vary.

4. Give two reasons explaining why a scientist maintains detailed records while doing research?

Possible answers: They need to be able to prove their conclusions. If the records are not carefully maintained, the conclusions may be wrong.

Fill in the circle next to the best answer.

5. Which tool would be used to measure a small amount of liquid for an experiment?

Ⓐ a crucible   ● a graduated cylinder
Ⓑ a beaker   Ⓓ a Petri dish

Assessment

Write *true* or *false*.

1. **true** An experiment always tests a hypothesis.
2. **false** A scientist makes a prediction based on the results of the experiment.
3. **true** Experiments need to be controlled to make sure they are fair.
4. **false** It is important to change at least two variables during an experiment.
5. **true** All data needs to be carefully recorded during an experiment.

Use each word in a sentence to explain its meaning.

dependent variable: **Answers will vary.**

independent variable: **Answers will vary.**

controlled variable: **Answers will vary.**

Write **S** in front of each rule that shows a safe lab practice.

S Wear safety glasses when you are working with glass, heat, or chemicals.
____ Dispose of all liquids in the lab sink when you are done.
____ Look down into the opening of a heating container to watch the reaction.
S Wash your hands before and after conducting a lab experiment.
S Baggy clothes should be avoided on lab days.
____ Place heated glassware into cool water immediately to easily remove residue.
S Horsing around should be avoided.

Should you read the entire set of instructions before beginning an experiment? Why or why not?

Possible answers: Yes, you should read the instructions. You need to make sure you have all the materials called for. You also need to know how to set up the experiment to complete it.

Day #1 · Day #2 · Day #3 · Day #4

Assessment # 4

Complete the page.

1. Sam noticed that a bronze statue in the park was turning green. He wants to find out why. What should Sam do before stating a hypothesis?

Possible answer: He should talk to park officials to see if they have sprayed chemicals and observe other statues.

2. In planning the experiment, what three materials might Sam need?

Possible answers: He might need bronze samples, goggles, hand lens, rainwater, insect sprays, or water.

3. Describe an experiment Sam can do to find out why the bronze statue is changing color.

Answers will vary.

4. What is the variable in the experiment?

Answers will vary.

Assessment

Answer Key

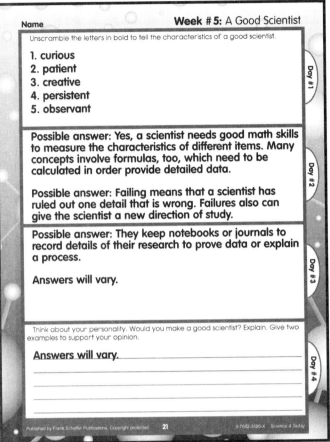

Unscramble the letters in bold to tell the characteristics of a good scientist.

1. curious
2. patient
3. creative
4. persistent
5. observant

Possible answer: Yes, a scientist needs good math skills to measure the characteristics of different items. Many concepts involve formulas, too, which need to be calculated in order provide detailed data.

Possible answer: Failing means that a scientist has ruled out one detail that is wrong. Failures also can give the scientist a new direction of study.

Possible answer: They keep notebooks or journals to record details of their research to prove data or explain a process.

Answers will vary.

Think about your personality. Would you make a good scientist? Explain. Give two examples to support your opinion.

Answers will vary.

Day #1

Day #2

Day #3

Day #4

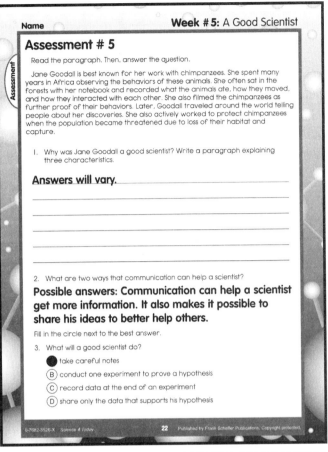

Assessment # 5

Read the paragraph. Then, answer the question.

Jane Goodall is best known for her work with chimpanzees. She spent many years in Africa observing the behaviors of these animals. She often sat in the forests with her notebook and recorded what the animals ate, how they moved, and how they interacted with each other. She also filmed the chimpanzees as further proof of their behaviors. Later, Goodall traveled around the world telling people about her discoveries. She also actively worked to protect chimpanzees when the population became threatened due to loss of their habitat and capture.

1. Why was Jane Goodall a good scientist? Write a paragraph explaining three characteristics.

Answers will vary.

2. What are two ways that communication can help a scientist?

Possible answers: Communication can help a scientist get more information. It also makes it possible to share his ideas to better help others.

Fill in the circle next to the best answer.

3. What will a good scientist do?
- ● take careful notes
- Ⓑ conduct one experiment to prove a hypothesis
- Ⓒ record data at the end of an experiment
- Ⓓ share only the data that supports his hypothesis

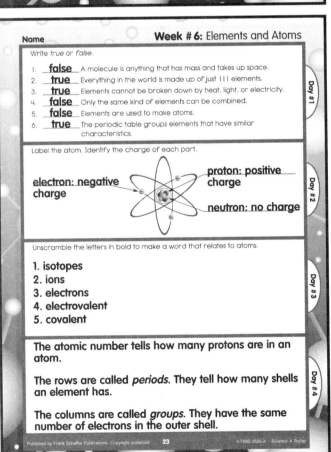

Write *true* or *false*.

1. **false** A molecule is anything that has mass and takes up space.
2. **true** Everything in the world is made up of just 111 elements.
3. **true** Elements cannot be broken down by heat, light, or electricity.
4. **false** Only the same kind of elements can be combined.
5. **false** Elements are used to make atoms.
6. **true** The periodic table groups elements that have similar characteristics.

Label the atom. Identify the charge of each part.

electron: negative charge

proton: positive charge

neutron: no charge

Unscramble the letters in bold to make a word that relates to atoms.

1. isotopes
2. ions
3. electrons
4. electrovalent
5. covalent

The atomic number tells how many protons are in an atom.

The rows are called *periods*. They tell how many shells an element has.

The columns are called *groups*. They have the same number of electrons in the outer shell.

Day #1

Day #2

Day #3

Day #4

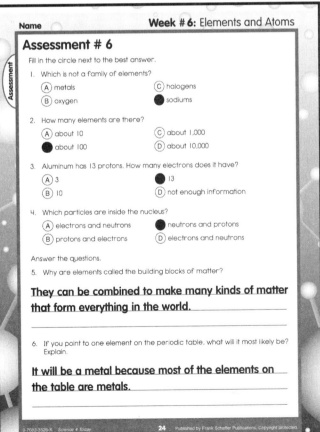

Assessment # 6

Fill in the circle next to the best answer.

1. Which is not a family of elements?
- Ⓐ metals
- Ⓒ halogens
- Ⓑ oxygen
- ● sodiums

2. How many elements are there?
- Ⓐ about 10
- Ⓒ about 1,000
- ● about 100
- Ⓓ about 10,000

3. Aluminum has 13 protons. How many electrons does it have?
- Ⓐ 3
- ● 13
- Ⓑ 10
- Ⓓ not enough information

4. Which particles are inside the nucleus?
- Ⓐ electrons and neutrons
- ● neutrons and protons
- Ⓑ protons and electrons
- Ⓓ electrons and neutrons

Answer the questions.

5. Why are elements called the building blocks of matter?

They can be combined to make many kinds of matter that form everything in the world.

6. If you point to one element on the periodic table, what will it most likely be? Explain.

It will be a metal because most of the elements on the table are metals.

Answer Key

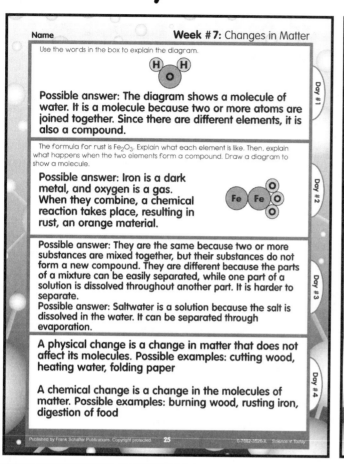

Use the words in the box to explain the diagram.

Day #1

Possible answer: The diagram shows a molecule of water. It is a molecule because two or more atoms are joined together. Since there are different elements, it is also a compound.

The formula for rust is Fe_2O_3. Explain what each element is like. Then, explain what happens when the two elements form a compound. Draw a diagram to show a molecule.

Day #2

Possible answer: Iron is a dark metal, and oxygen is a gas. When they combine, a chemical reaction takes place, resulting in rust, an orange material.

Day #3

Possible answer: They are the same because two or more substances are mixed together, but their substances do not form a new compound. They are different because the parts of a mixture can be easily separated, while one part of a solution is dissolved throughout another part. It is harder to separate.

Possible answer: Saltwater is a solution because the salt is dissolved in the water. It can be separated through evaporation.

Day #4

A physical change is a change in matter that does not affect its molecules. Possible examples: cutting wood, heating water, folding paper

A chemical change is a change in the molecules of matter. Possible examples: burning wood, rusting iron, digestion of food

---

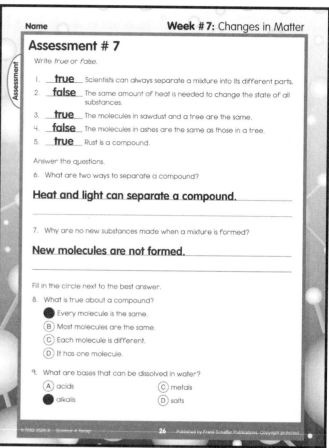

Assessment # 7

Write *true* or *false*.

1. **true** Scientists can always separate a mixture into its different parts.
2. **false** The same amount of heat is needed to change the state of all substances.
3. **true** The molecules in sawdust and a tree are the same.
4. **false** The molecules in ashes are the same as those in a tree.
5. **true** Rust is a compound.

Answer the questions.

6. What are two ways to separate a compound?

Heat and light can separate a compound.

7. Why are no new substances made when a mixture is formed?

New molecules are not formed.

Fill in the circle next to the best answer.

8. What is true about a compound?
   - ● Every molecule is the same.
   - Ⓑ Most molecules are the same.
   - Ⓒ Each molecule is different.
   - Ⓓ It has one molecule.

9. What are bases that can be dissolved in water?
   - Ⓐ acids   Ⓒ metals
   - ● alkalis   Ⓓ salts

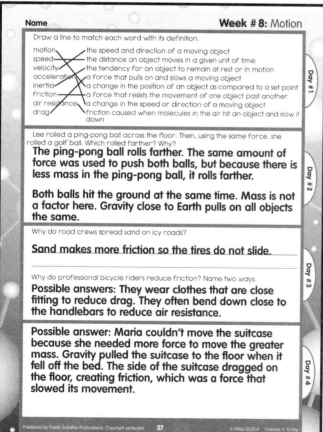

Draw a line to match each word with its definition.

Day #1

motion — the speed and direction of a moving object
speed — the distance an object moves in a given unit of time
velocity — the tendency for an object to remain at rest or in motion
acceleration — a force that pulls on and slows a moving object
inertia — a change in the position of an object as compared to a set point
friction — a force that resists the movement of one object past another
air resistance — a change in the speed or direction of a moving object
drag — friction caused when molecules in the air hit an object and slow it down

Lee rolled a ping-pong ball across the floor. Then, using the same force, she rolled a golf ball. Which rolled farther? Why?

Day #2

The ping-pong ball rolls farther. The same amount of force was used to push both balls, but because there is less mass in the ping-pong ball, it rolls farther.

Both balls hit the ground at the same time. Mass is not a factor here. Gravity close to Earth pulls on all objects the same.

Why do road crews spread sand on icy roads?

Day #3

Sand makes more friction so the tires do not slide.

Why do professional bicycle riders reduce friction? Name two ways.

Possible answers: They wear clothes that are close fitting to reduce drag. They often bend down close to the handlebars to reduce air resistance.

Day #4

Possible answer: Maria couldn't move the suitcase because she needed more force to move the greater mass. Gravity pulled the suitcase to the floor when it fell off the bed. The side of the suitcase dragged on the floor, creating friction, which was a force that slowed its movement.

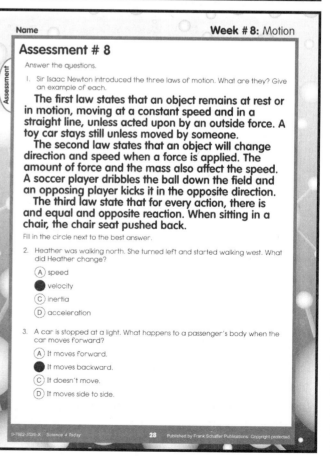

Assessment # 8

Answer the questions.

1. Sir Isaac Newton introduced the three laws of motion. What are they? Give an example of each.

The first law states that an object remains at rest or in motion, moving at a constant speed and in a straight line, unless acted upon by an outside force. A toy car stays still unless moved by someone.

The second law states that an object will change direction and speed when a force is applied. The amount of force and the mass also affect the speed. A soccer player dribbles the ball down the field and an opposing player kicks it in the opposite direction.

The third law state that for every action, there is and equal and opposite reaction. When sitting in a chair, the chair seat pushed back.

Fill in the circle next to the best answer.

2. Heather was walking north. She turned left and started walking west. What did Heather change?
   - Ⓐ speed
   - ● velocity
   - Ⓒ inertia
   - Ⓓ acceleration

3. A car is stopped at a light. What happens to a passenger's body when the car moves forward?
   - Ⓐ It moves forward.
   - ● It moves backward.
   - Ⓒ It doesn't move.
   - Ⓓ It moves side to side.

Answer Key

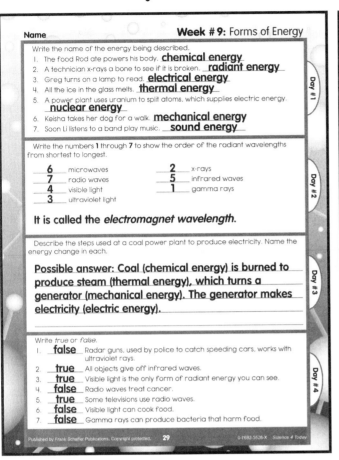

Write the name of the energy being described.
1. The food Rod ate powers his body. **chemical energy**
2. A technician x-rays a bone to see if it is broken. **radiant energy**
3. Greg turns on a lamp to read. **electrical energy**
4. All the ice in the glass melts. **thermal energy**
5. A power plant uses uranium to split atoms, which supplies electric energy. **nuclear energy**
6. Keisha takes her dog for a walk. **mechanical energy**
7. Soon Li listens to a band play music. **sound energy**

Day #1

Write the numbers **1** through **7** to show the order of the radiant wavelengths from shortest to longest.

6 microwaves   **2** x-rays
7 radio waves   **5** infrared waves
4 visible light   **1** gamma rays
3 ultraviolet light

It is called the *electromagnet wavelength*.

Day #2

Describe the steps used at a coal power plant to produce electricity. Name the energy change in each.

Possible answer: Coal (chemical energy) is burned to produce steam (thermal energy), which turns a generator (mechanical energy). The generator makes electricity (electric energy).

Day #3

Write *true* or *false*.
1. **false** Radar guns, used by police to catch speeding cars, works with ultraviolet rays.
2. **true** All objects give off infrared waves.
3. **true** Visible light is the only form of radiant energy you can see.
4. **false** Radio waves treat cancer.
5. **true** Some televisions use radio waves.
6. **false** Visible light can cook food.
7. **false** Gamma rays can produce bacteria that harm food.

Day #4

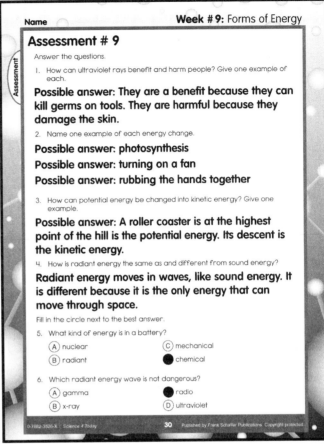

Assessment # 9

Answer the questions.
1. How can ultraviolet rays benefit and harm people? Give one example of each.

Possible answer: They are a benefit because they can kill germs on tools. They are harmful because they damage the skin.

2. Name one example of each energy change.

Possible answer: photosynthesis

Possible answer: turning on a fan

Possible answer: rubbing the hands together

3. How can potential energy be changed into kinetic energy? Give one example.

Possible answer: A roller coaster is at the highest point of the hill is the potential energy. Its descent is the kinetic energy.

4. How is radiant energy the same as and different from sound energy?

Radiant energy moves in waves, like sound energy. It is different because it is the only energy that can move through space.

Fill in the circle next to the best answer.
5. What kind of energy is in a battery?
   (A) nuclear   (C) mechanical
   (B) radiant   ● chemical

6. Which radiant energy wave is not dangerous?
   (A) gamma   ● radio
   (B) x-ray   (D) ultraviolet

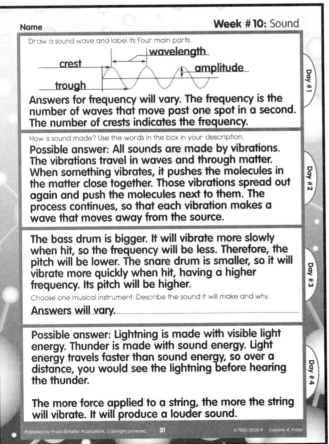

Draw a sound wave and label its four main parts.

wavelength
crest
amplitude
trough

Day #1

Answers for frequency will vary. The frequency is the number of waves that move past one spot in a second. The number of crests indicates the frequency.

How is sound made? Use the words in the box in your description.
Possible answer: All sounds are made by vibrations. The vibrations travel in waves and through matter. When something vibrates, it pushes the molecules in the matter close together. Those vibrations spread out again and push the molecules next to them. The process continues, so that each vibration makes a wave that moves away from the source.

Day #2

The bass drum is bigger. It will vibrate more slowly when hit, so the frequency will be less. Therefore, the pitch will be lower. The snare drum is smaller, so it will vibrate more quickly when hit, having a higher frequency. Its pitch will be higher.

Choose one musical instrument. Describe the sound it will make and why.
Answers will vary.

Day #3

Possible answer: Lightning is made with visible light energy. Thunder is made with sound energy. Light energy travels faster than sound energy, so over a distance, you would see the lightning before hearing the thunder.

The more force applied to a string, the more the string will vibrate. It will produce a louder sound.

Day #4

Assessment # 10

Look at the chart. Then, fill in the circle next to the best answer.

Animal	Approximate Range (Hz)
dog	67-45,000
human being	64-23,000
elephant	16-12,000
porpoise	75-150,000
mouse	1,000-91,000

1. Which animal can hear the highest pitched sound?
   (A) dog   (C) human being
   (B) elephant   ● porpoise

2. How many vibrations must an object make for a human being to hear it?
   (A) 10   ● 200
   (B) 60   (D) 24,000

3. An object is producing 38,000 Hz. Which animal cannot hear it?
   (A) mouse   (C) porpoise
   ● elephant   (D) dog

Answer the questions.
4. What is compression and rarefaction in a wave? Label the diagram to show each.

compression   rarefaction

Compression is when the molecules moving in a sound wave are close together and denser due to the vibrations. Rarefaction is when the molecules are spread out.

Answer Key

Name

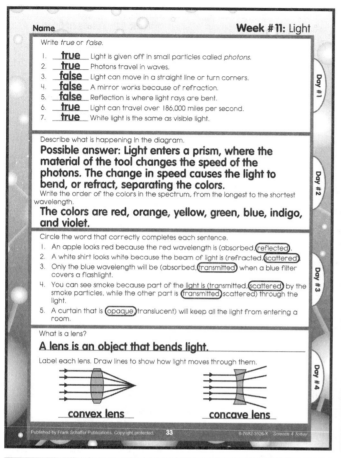

Week #11: Light

Write *true* or *false*.

1. **true** Light is given off in small particles called *photons*.
2. **true** Photons travel in waves.
3. **false** Light can move in a straight line or turn corners.
4. **false** A mirror works because of refraction.
5. **false** Reflection is where light rays are bent.
6. **true** Light can travel over 186,000 miles per second.
7. **true** White light is the same as visible light.

Day #1

Describe what is happening in the diagram.

Possible answer: Light enters a prism, where the material of the tool changes the speed of the photons. The change in speed causes the light to bend, or refract, separating the colors.

Write the order of the colors in the spectrum, from the longest to the shortest wavelength.

The colors are red, orange, yellow, green, blue, indigo, and violet.

Day #2

Circle the word that correctly completes each sentence.

1. An apple looks red because the red wavelength is (absorbed, (reflected)).
2. A white shirt looks white because the beam of light is (refracted, (scattered)).
3. Only the blue wavelength will be (absorbed, (transmitted)) when a blue filter covers a flashlight.
4. You can see smoke because part of the light is (transmitted, (scattered)) by the smoke particles, while the other part is ((transmitted), scattered) through the light.
5. A curtain that is ((opaque), translucent) will keep all the light from entering a room.

Day #3

What is a lens?

A lens is an object that bends light.

Label each lens. Draw lines to show how light moves through them.

convex lens   **concave lens**

Day #4

Published by Frank Schaffer Publications. Copyright protected.   **33**   0-7682-3526-X   *Science 4 Today*

Name

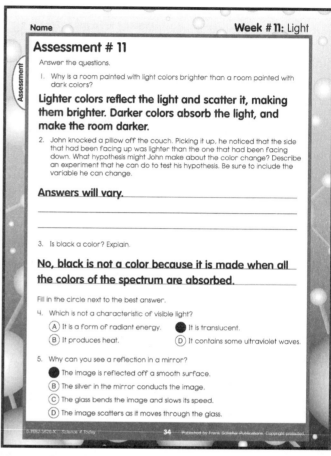

Week #11: Light

Assessment

Assessment # 11

Answer the questions.

1. Why is a room painted with light colors brighter than a room painted with dark colors?

Lighter colors reflect the light and scatter it, making them brighter. Darker colors absorb the light, and make the room darker.

2. John knocked a pillow off the couch. Picking it up, he noticed that the side that had been facing up was lighter than the one that had been facing down. What hypothesis might John make about the color change? Describe an experiment that he can do to test his hypothesis. Be sure to include the variable he can change.

Answers will vary.

3. Is black a color? Explain.

No, black is not a color because it is made when all the colors of the spectrum are absorbed.

Fill in the circle next to the best answer.

4. Which is not a characteristic of visible light?
   - (A) It is a form of radiant energy.
   - ● It is translucent.
   - (B) It produces heat.
   - (D) It contains some ultraviolet waves.

5. Why can you see a reflection in a mirror?
   - ● The image is reflected off a smooth surface.
   - (B) The silver in the mirror conducts the image.
   - (C) The glass bends the image and slows its speed.
   - (D) The image scatters as it moves through the glass.

0-7682-3526-X   *Science 4 Today*   **34**   Published by Frank Schaffer Publications. Copyright protected.

Name

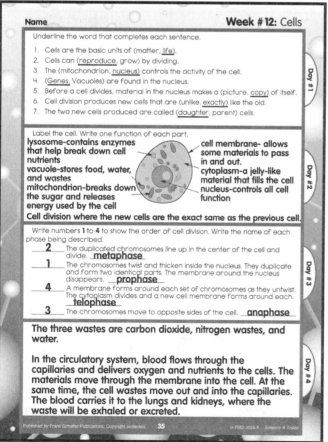

Week #12: Cells

Underline the word that completes each sentence.

1. Cells are the basic units of (matter, life).
2. Cells can (reproduce, grow) by dividing.
3. The (mitochondrion, nucleus) controls the activity of the cell.
4. (Genes, Vacuoles) are found in the nucleus.
5. Before a cell divides, material in the nucleus makes a (picture, copy) of itself.
6. Cell division produces new cells that are (unlike, exactly) like the old.
7. The two new cells produced are called (daughter, parent) cells.

Day #1

Label the cell. Write one function of each part.

lysosome-contains enzymes that help break down cell nutrients
vacuole-stores food, water, and wastes
mitochondrion-breaks down the sugar and releases energy used by the cell

cell membrane- allows some materials to pass in and out.
cytoplasm-a jelly-like material that fills the cell
nucleus-controls all cell function

Cell division where the new cells are the exact same as the previous cell.

Day #2

Write numbers **1** to **4** to show the order of cell division. Write the name of each phase being described.

2 The duplicated chromosomes line up in the center of the cell and divide. **metaphase**

1 The chromosomes twist and thicken inside the nucleus. They duplicate and form two identical parts. The membrane around the nucleus disappears. **prophase**

4 A membrane forms around each set of chromosomes as they untwist. The cytoplasm divides and a new cell membrane forms around each. **telophase**

3 The chromosomes move to opposite sides of the cell. **anaphase**

Day #3

The three wastes are carbon dioxide, nitrogen wastes, and water.

In the circulatory system, blood flows through the capillaries and delivers oxygen and nutrients to the cells. The materials move through the membrane into the cell. At the same time, the cell wastes move out and into the capillaries. The blood carries it to the lungs and kidneys, where the waste will be exhaled or excreted.

Day #4

Published by Frank Schaffer Publications. Copyright protected.   **35**   0-7682-3526-X   *Science 4 Today*

Name

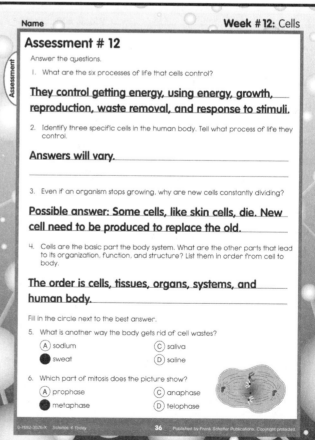

Week #12: Cells

Assessment

Assessment # 12

Answer the questions.

1. What are the six processes of life that cells control?

They control getting energy, using energy, growth, reproduction, waste removal, and response to stimuli.

2. Identify three specific cells in the human body. Tell what process of life they control.

Answers will vary.

3. Even if an organism stops growing, why are new cells constantly dividing?

Possible answer: Some cells, like skin cells, die. New cell need to be produced to replace the old.

4. Cells are the basic part the body system. What are the other parts that lead to its organization, function, and structure? List them in order from cell to body.

The order is cells, tissues, organs, systems, and human body.

Fill in the circle next to the best answer.

5. What is another way the body gets rid of cell wastes?
   - (A) sodium
   - (C) saliva
   - ● sweat
   - (D) saline

6. Which part of mitosis does the picture show?
   - (A) prophase
   - (C) anaphase
   - ● metaphase
   - (D) telophase

0-7682-3526-X   *Science 4 Today*   **36**   Published by Frank Schaffer Publications. Copyright protected.

Answer Key

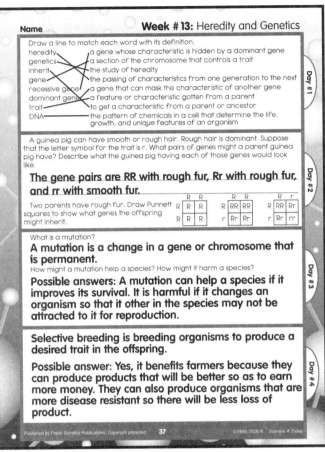

Week # 13: Heredity and Genetics

Day #1

Draw a line to match each word with its definition.

heredity — a gene whose characteristic is hidden by a dominant gene
genetics — a section of the chromosome that controls a trait
inherit — the study of heredity
gene — the passing of characteristics from one generation to the next
recessive gene — a gene that can mask the characteristic of another gene
dominant gene — a feature or characteristic gotten from a parent
trait — to get a characteristic from a parent or ancestor
DNA — the pattern of chemicals in a cell that determine the life, growth, and unique features of an organism

Day #2

A guinea pig can have smooth or rough hair. Rough hair is dominant. Suppose that the letter symbol for the trait is r. What pairs of genes might a parent guinea pig have? Describe what the guinea pig having each of those genes would look like.

The gene pairs are RR with rough fur, Rr with rough fur, and rr with smooth fur.

Two parents have rough fur. Draw Punnett squares to show what genes the offspring might inherit.

	R	R
R	R	R
R	R	R

	R	R
R	RR	RR
r	Rr	Rr

	R	r
R	RR	Rr
r	Rr	Rr

Day #3

What is a mutation?

A mutation is a change in a gene or chromosome that is permanent.

How might a mutation help a species? How might it harm a species?

Possible answers: A mutation can help a species if it improves its survival. It is harmful if it changes an organism so that it other in the species may not be attracted to it for reproduction.

Day #4

Selective breeding is breeding organisms to produce a desired trait in the offspring.

Possible answer: Yes, it benefits farmers because they can produce products that will be better so as to earn more money. They can also produce organisms that are more disease resistant so there will be less loss of product.

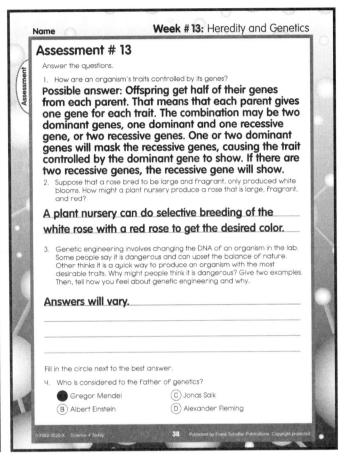

Week # 13: Heredity and Genetics

Assessment

Assessment # 13

Answer the questions.

1. How are an organism's traits controlled by its genes?

Possible answer: Offspring get half of their genes from each parent. That means that each parent gives one gene for each trait. The combination may be two dominant genes, one dominant and one recessive gene, or two recessive genes. One or two dominant genes will mask the recessive genes, causing the trait controlled by the dominant gene to show. If there are two recessive genes, the recessive gene will show.

2. Suppose that a rose bred to be large and fragrant, only produced white blooms. How might a plant nursery produce a rose that is large, fragrant, and red?

A plant nursery can do selective breeding of the white rose with a red rose to get the desired color.

3. Genetic engineering involves changing the DNA of an organism in the lab. Some people say it is dangerous and can upset the balance of nature. Other thinks it is a quick way to produce an organism with the most desirable traits. Why might people think it is dangerous? Give two examples. Then, tell how you feel about genetic engineering and why.

Answers will vary. _____

Fill in the circle next to the best answer.

4. Who is considered to the father of genetics?
   ● Gregor Mendel
   Ⓒ Jonas Salk
   Ⓑ Albert Einstein
   Ⓓ Alexander Fleming

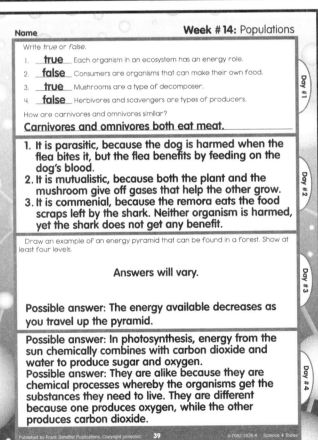

Week # 14: Populations

Day #1

Write *true* or *false*.

1. **true** Each organism in an ecosystem has an energy role.
2. **false** Consumers are organisms that can make their own food.
3. **true** Mushrooms are a type of decomposer.
4. **false** Herbivores and scavengers are types of producers.

How are carnivores and omnivores similar?

Carnivores and omnivores both eat meat.

Day #2

1. **It is parasitic, because the dog is harmed when the flea bites it, but the flea benefits by feeding on the dog's blood.**
2. **It is mutualistic, because both the plant and the mushroom give off gases that help the other grow.**
3. **It is commenial, because the remora eats the food scraps left by the shark. Neither organism is harmed, yet the shark does not get any benefit.**

Day #3

Draw an example of an energy pyramid that can be found in a forest. Show at least four levels.

Answers will vary.

Possible answer: The energy available decreases as you travel up the pyramid.

Day #4

Possible answer: In photosynthesis, energy from the sun chemically combines with carbon dioxide and water to produce sugar and oxygen.

Possible answer: They are alike because they are chemical processes whereby the organisms get the substances they need to live. They are different because one produces oxygen, while the other produces carbon dioxide.

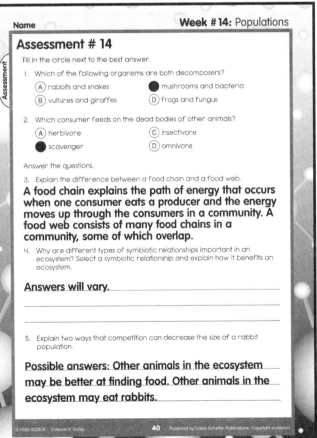

Week # 14: Populations

Assessment

Assessment # 14

Fill in the circle next to the best answer.

1. Which of the following organisms are both decomposers?
   Ⓐ rabbits and snakes
   ● mushrooms and bacteria
   Ⓑ vultures and giraffes
   Ⓓ frogs and fungus

2. Which consumer feeds on the dead bodies of other animals?
   Ⓐ herbivore
   Ⓒ insectivore
   ● scavenger
   Ⓓ omnivore

Answer the questions.

3. Explain the difference between a food chain and a food web.

A food chain explains the path of energy that occurs when one consumer eats a producer and the energy moves up through the consumers in a community. A food web consists of many food chains in a community, some of which overlap.

4. Why are different types of symbiotic relationships important in an ecosystem? Select a symbiotic relationship and explain how it benefits an ecosystem.

Answers will vary. _____

5. Explain two ways that competition can decrease the size of a rabbit population.

Possible answers: Other animals in the ecosystem may be better at finding food. Other animals in the ecosystem may eat rabbits.

Answer Key

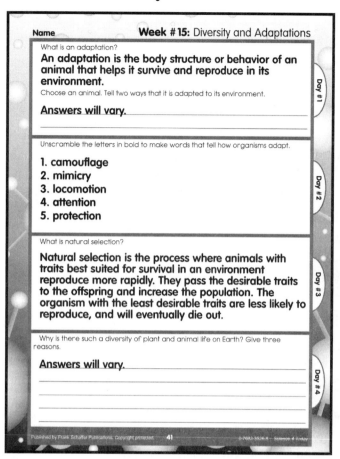

What is an adaptation?

An adaptation is the body structure or behavior of an animal that helps it survive and reproduce in its environment.

Choose an animal. Tell two ways that it is adapted to its environment.

Answers will vary.

Day #1

Unscramble the letters in bold to make words that tell how organisms adapt.

1. **camouflage**
2. **mimicry**
3. **locomotion**
4. **attention**
5. **protection**

Day #2

What is natural selection?

Natural selection is the process where animals with traits best suited for survival in an environment reproduce more rapidly. They pass the desirable traits to the offspring and increase the population. The organism with the least desirable traits are less likely to reproduce, and will eventually die out.

Day #3

Why is there such a diversity of plant and animal life on Earth? Give three reasons.

Answers will vary.

Day #4

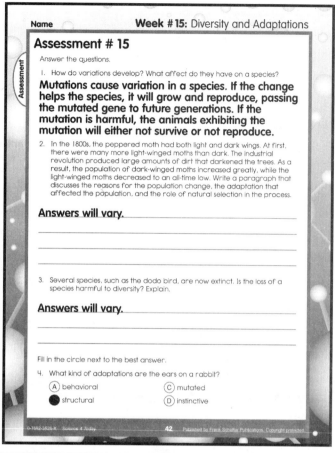

Assessment

Assessment # 15

Answer the questions.

1. How do variations develop? What affect do they have on a species?

Mutations cause variation in a species. If the change helps the species, it will grow and reproduce, passing the mutated gene to future generations. If the mutation is harmful, the animals exhibiting the mutation will either not survive or not reproduce.

2. In the 1800s, the peppered moth had both light and dark wings. At first, there were many more light-winged moths than dark. The industrial revolution produced large amounts of dirt that darkened the trees. As a result, the population of dark-winged moths increased greatly, while the light-winged moths decreased to an all-time low. Write a paragraph that discusses the reasons for the population change, the adaptation that affected the population, and the role of natural selection in the process.

Answers will vary.

3. Several species, such as the dodo bird, are now extinct. Is the loss of a species harmful to diversity? Explain.

Answers will vary.

Fill in the circle next to the best answer.

4. What kind of adaptations are the ears on a rabbit?
   - (A) behavioral
   - (C) mutated
   - ● structural
   - (D) instinctive

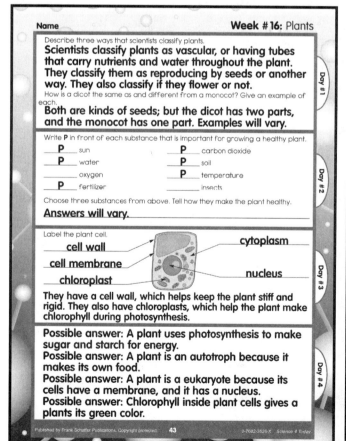

Describe three ways that scientists classify plants.

Scientists classify plants as vascular, or having tubes that carry nutrients and water throughout the plant. They classify them as reproducing by seeds or another way. They also classify if they flower or not.

How is a dicot the same as and different from a monocot? Give an example of each.

Both are kinds of seeds; but the dicot has two parts, and the monocot has one part. Examples will vary.

Day #1

Write **P** in front of each substance that is important for growing a healthy plant.

P sun   **P** carbon dioxide
P water   **P** soil
_____ oxygen   **P** temperature
P fertilizer   _____ insects

Choose three substances from above. Tell how they make the plant healthy.

Answers will vary.

Day #2

Label the plant cell.

cell wall   **cytoplasm**
cell membrane
chloroplast   **nucleus**

They have a cell wall, which helps keep the plant stiff and rigid. They also have chloroplasts, which help the plant make chlorophyll during photosynthesis.

Day #3

Possible answer: A plant uses photosynthesis to make sugar and starch for energy.
Possible answer: A plant is an autotroph because it makes its own food.
Possible answer: A plant is a eukaryote because its cells have a membrane, and it has a nucleus.
Possible answer: Chlorophyll inside plant cells gives a plants its green color.

Day #4

Assessment

Assessment # 16

Fill in the circle next to the best answer.

1. What is the main source of energy for plants?
   - ● sugar
   - (C) decomposers
   - (B) nutrients
   - (D) oxygen

2. Which is not a way to grow plants without seeds?
   - (A) Roots are divided and replanted.
   - ● A leaf is replanted.
   - (C) The stem of one plant is joined to an established root system.
   - (D) A piece of a small plant is cut off and replanted.

Answer the questions.

3. What are three ways that plants interact with their non-living environment?

Possible answers: They interact with the soil, which provides support to keep the plant anchored in the ground. The soil also provides nutrients that keep it healthy. They interact with the sun to get the energy needed for photosynthesis. They interact with water to keep fluid flowing through their system and also aid photosynthesis.

4. What is the nitrogen cycle? What parts do plants play in it?

The nitrogen cycle is the process where the nitrogen gas that is unusable is changed to a form that organisms can use. Some bacteria in plant roots can change nitrogen gas into a compound. Plants use the compounds to make protein. Decomposers return compounds to the soil when the get the energy from dead plants.

5. Choose one plant. Tell three ways it is adapted to its environment.

Answers will vary.

Answer Key

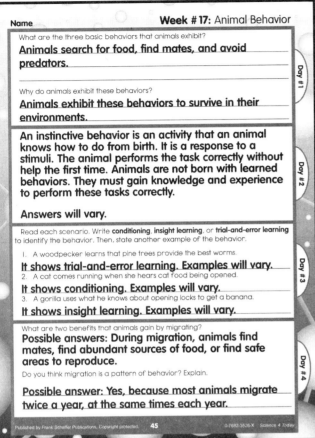

Name   **Week #17:** Animal Behavior

Day #1

What are the three basic behaviors that animals exhibit?

Animals search for food, find mates, and avoid predators.

Why do animals exhibit these behaviors?

Animals exhibit these behaviors to survive in their environments.

Day #2

An instinctive behavior is an activity that an animal knows how to do from birth. It is a response to a stimuli. The animal performs the task correctly without help the first time. Animals are not born with learned behaviors. They must gain knowledge and experience to perform these tasks correctly.

Answers will vary.

Day #3

Read each scenario. Write **conditioning**, **insight learning**, or **trial-and-error learning** to identify the behavior. Then, state another example of the behavior.

1. A woodpecker learns that pine trees provide the best worms.

It shows trial-and-error learning. Examples will vary.

2. A cat comes running when she hears cat food being opened.

It shows conditioning. Examples will vary.

3. A gorilla uses what he knows about opening locks to get a banana.

It shows insight learning. Examples will vary.

Day #4

What are two benefits that animals gain by migrating?

Possible answers: During migration, animals find mates, find abundant sources of food, or find safe areas to reproduce.

Do you think migration is a pattern of behavior? Explain.

Possible answer: Yes, because most animals migrate twice a year, at the same times each year.

Published by Frank Schaffer Publications. Copyright protected.   45   0-7682-3526-X   Science 4 Today

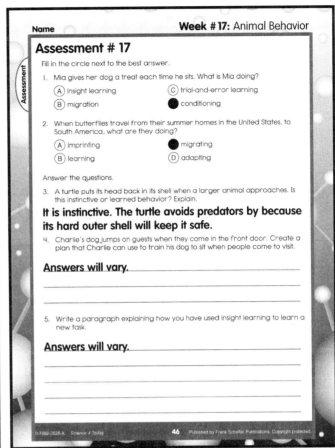

Name   **Week #17:** Animal Behavior

Assessment

Assessment # 17

Fill in the circle next to the best answer.

1. Mia gives her dog a treat each time he sits. What is Mia doing?
   - Ⓐ insight learning
   - Ⓒ trial-and-error learning
   - Ⓑ migration
   - ⬤ conditioning

2. When butterflies travel from their summer homes in the United States, to South America, what are they doing?
   - Ⓐ imprinting
   - ⬤ migrating
   - Ⓑ learning
   - Ⓓ adapting

Answer the questions.

3. A turtle puts its head back in its shell when a larger animal approaches. Is this instinctive or learned behavior? Explain.

It is instinctive. The turtle avoids predators by because its hard outer shell will keep it safe.

4. Charlie's dog jumps on guests when they come in the front door. Create a plan that Charlie can use to train his dog to sit when people come to visit.

Answers will vary.

5. Write a paragraph explaining how you have used insight learning to learn a new task.

Answers will vary.

0-7682-3526-X   Science 4 Today   46   Published by Frank Schaffer Publications. Copyright protected.

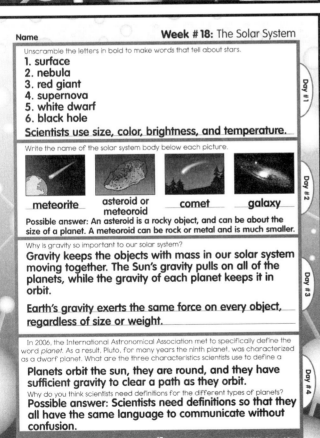

Name   **Week #18:** The Solar System

Day #1

Unscramble the letters in bold to make words that tell about stars.

1. surface
2. nebula
3. red giant
4. supernova
5. white dwarf
6. black hole

Scientists use size, color, brightness, and temperature.

Day #2

Write the name of the solar system body below each picture.

meteorite | asteroid or meteoroid | comet | galaxy

Possible answer: An asteroid is a rocky object, and can be about the size of a planet. A meteoroid can be rock or metal and is much smaller.

Day #3

Why is gravity so important to our solar system?

Gravity keeps the objects with mass in our solar system moving together. The Sun's gravity pulls on all of the planets, while the gravity of each planet keeps it in orbit.

Earth's gravity exerts the same force on every object, regardless of size or weight.

Day #4

In 2006, the International Astronomical Association met to specifically define the word *planet*. As a result, Pluto, for many years the ninth planet, was characterized as a dwarf planet. What are the three characteristics scientists use to define a

Planets orbit the sun, they are round, and they have sufficient gravity to clear a path as they orbit.

Why do you think scientists need definitions for the different types of planets?

Possible answer: Scientists need definitions so that they all have the same language to communicate without confusion.

Published by Frank Schaffer Publications. Copyright protected.   47   0-7682-3526-X   Science 4 Today

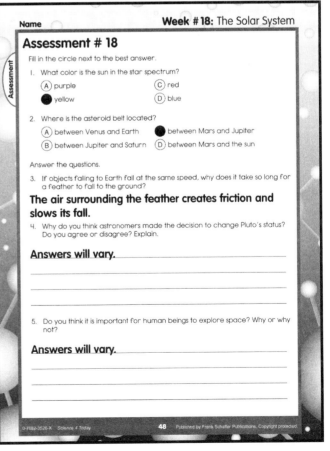

Name   **Week #18:** The Solar System

Assessment

Assessment # 18

Fill in the circle next to the best answer.

1. What color is the sun in the star spectrum?
   - Ⓐ purple
   - Ⓒ red
   - ⬤ yellow
   - Ⓓ blue

2. Where is the asteroid belt located?
   - Ⓐ between Venus and Earth
   - ⬤ between Mars and Jupiter
   - Ⓑ between Jupiter and Saturn
   - Ⓓ between Mars and the sun

Answer the questions.

3. If objects falling to Earth fall at the same speed, why does it take so long for a feather to fall to the ground?

The air surrounding the feather creates friction and slows its fall.

4. Why do you think astronomers made the decision to change Pluto's status? Do you agree or disagree? Explain.

Answers will vary.

5. Do you think it is important for human beings to explore space? Why or why not?

Answers will vary.

0-7682-3526-X   Science 4 Today   48   Published by Frank Schaffer Publications. Copyright protected.

Answer Key

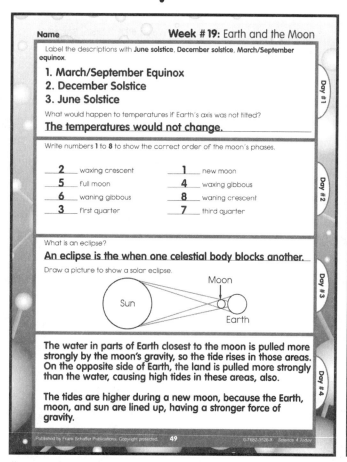

Name   **Week #19:** Earth and the Moon

Label the descriptions with **June solstice, December solstice, March/September equinox.**

1. March/September Equinox
2. December Solstice
3. June Solstice

What would happen to temperatures if Earth's axis was not tilted?

The temperatures would not change.

Write numbers **1** to **8** to show the correct order of the moon's phases.

2 waxing crescent   **1** new moon
5 full moon   **4** waxing gibbous
6 waning gibbous   **8** waning crescent
3 first quarter   **7** third quarter

What is an eclipse?

An eclipse is the when one celestial body blocks another.

Draw a picture to show a solar eclipse.

Sun   Moon   Earth

The water in parts of Earth closest to the moon is pulled more strongly by the moon's gravity, so the tide rises in those areas. On the opposite side of Earth, the land is pulled more strongly than the water, causing high tides in these areas, also.

The tides are higher during a new moon, because the Earth, moon, and sun are lined up, having a stronger force of gravity.

Day #1 · Day #2 · Day #3 · Day #4

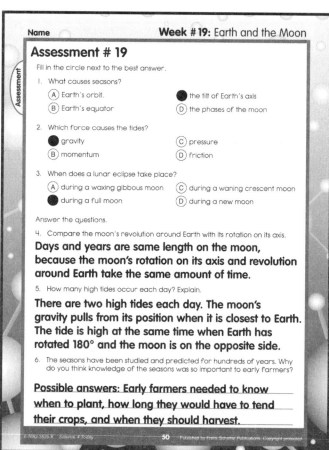

Name   **Week #19:** Earth and the Moon

Assessment # 19

Fill in the circle next to the best answer.

1. What causes seasons?
   A Earth's orbit.   ● the tilt of Earth's axis
   B Earth's equator   D the phases of the moon

2. Which force causes the tides?
   ● gravity   C pressure
   B momentum   D friction

3. When does a lunar eclipse take place?
   A during a waxing gibbous moon   C during a waning crescent moon
   ● during a full moon   D during a new moon

Answer the questions.

4. Compare the moon's revolution around Earth with its rotation on its axis.

Days and years are same length on the moon, because the moon's rotation on its axis and revolution around Earth take the same amount of time.

5. How many high tides occur each day? Explain.

There are two high tides each day. The moon's gravity pulls from its position when it is closest to Earth. The tide is high at the same time when Earth has rotated 180° and the moon is on the opposite side.

6. The seasons have been studied and predicted for hundreds of years. Why do you think knowledge of the seasons was so important to early farmers?

Possible answers: Early farmers needed to know when to plant, how long they would have to tend their crops, and when they should harvest.

Assessment

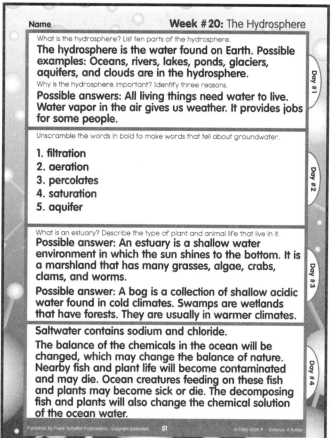

Name   **Week #20:** The Hydrosphere

What is the hydrosphere? List ten parts of the hydrosphere.

The hydrosphere is the water found on Earth. Possible examples: Oceans, rivers, lakes, ponds, glaciers, aquifers, and clouds are in the hydrosphere.

Why is the hydrosphere important? Identify three reasons.

Possible answers: All living things need water to live. Water vapor in the air gives us weather. It provides jobs for some people.

Unscramble the words in bold to make words that tell about groundwater.

1. filtration
2. aeration
3. percolates
4. saturation
5. aquifer

What is an estuary? Describe the type of plant and animal life that live in it.

Possible answer: An estuary is a shallow water environment in which the sun shines to the bottom. It is a marshland that has many grasses, algae, crabs, clams, and worms.

Possible answer: A bog is a collection of shallow acidic water found in cold climates. Swamps are wetlands that have forests. They are usually in warmer climates.

Saltwater contains sodium and chloride.

The balance of the chemicals in the ocean will be changed, which may change the balance of nature. Nearby fish and plant life will become contaminated and may die. Ocean creatures feeding on these fish and plants may become sick or die. The decomposing fish and plants will also change the chemical solution of the ocean water.

Day #1 · Day #2 · Day #3 · Day #4

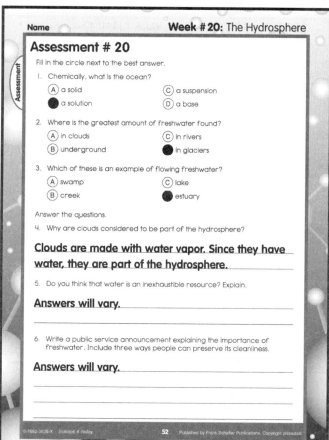

Name   **Week #20:** The Hydrosphere

Assessment # 20

Fill in the circle next to the best answer.

1. Chemically, what is the ocean?
   A a solid   C a suspension
   ● a solution   D a base

2. Where is the greatest amount of freshwater found?
   A in clouds   C in rivers
   B underground   ● in glaciers

3. Which of these is an example of flowing freshwater?
   A swamp   C lake
   B creek   ● estuary

Answer the questions.

4. Why are clouds considered to be part of the hydrosphere?

Clouds are made with water vapor. Since they have water, they are part of the hydrosphere.

5. Do you think that water is an inexhaustible resource? Explain.

Answers will vary.

6. Write a public service announcement explaining the importance of freshwater. Include three ways people can preserve its cleanliness.

Answers will vary.

Assessment

Answer Key

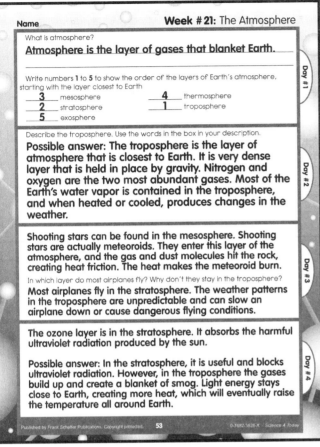

What is atmosphere?

Atmosphere is the layer of gases that blanket Earth.

Write numbers **1** to **5** to show the order of the layers of Earth's atmosphere, starting with the layer closest to Earth

3 mesosphere   **4** thermosphere
2 stratosphere   **1** troposphere
5 exosphere

Day #1

Describe the troposphere. Use the words in the box in your description.

Possible answer: The troposphere is the layer of atmosphere that is closest to Earth. It is very dense layer that is held in place by gravity. Nitrogen and oxygen are the two most abundant gases. Most of the Earth's water vapor is contained in the troposphere, and when heated or cooled, produces changes in the weather.

Day #2

Shooting stars can be found in the mesosphere. Shooting stars are actually meteoroids. They enter this layer of the atmosphere, and the gas and dust molecules hit the rock, creating heat friction. The heat makes the meteoroid burn.

In which layer do most airplanes fly? Why don't they stay in the troposphere?
Most airplanes fly in the stratosphere. The weather patterns in the troposphere are unpredictable and can slow an airplane down or cause dangerous flying conditions.

Day #3

The ozone layer is in the stratosphere. It absorbs the harmful ultraviolet radiation produced by the sun.

Possible answer: In the stratosphere, it is useful and blocks ultraviolet radiation. However, in the troposphere the gases build up and create a blanket of smog. Light energy stays close to Earth, creating more heat, which will eventually raise the temperature all around Earth.

Day #4

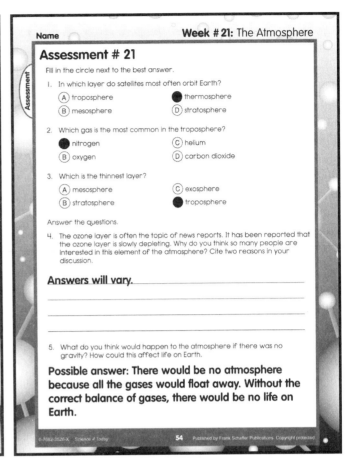

Assessment # 21

Fill in the circle next to the best answer.

1. In which layer do satellites most often orbit Earth?
   - (A) troposphere
   - ● thermosphere
   - (B) mesosphere
   - (D) stratosphere

2. Which gas is the most common in the troposphere?
   - ● nitrogen
   - (C) helium
   - (B) oxygen
   - (D) carbon dioxide

3. Which is the thinnest layer?
   - (A) mesosphere
   - (C) exosphere
   - (B) stratosphere
   - ● troposphere

Answer the questions.

4. The ozone layer is often the topic of news reports. It has been reported that the ozone layer is slowly depleting. Why do you think so many people are interested in this element of the atmosphere? Cite two reasons in your discussion.

Answers will vary.

5. What do you think would happen to the atmosphere if there was no gravity? How could this affect life on Earth.

Possible answer: There would be no atmosphere because all the gases would float away. Without the correct balance of gases, there would be no life on Earth.

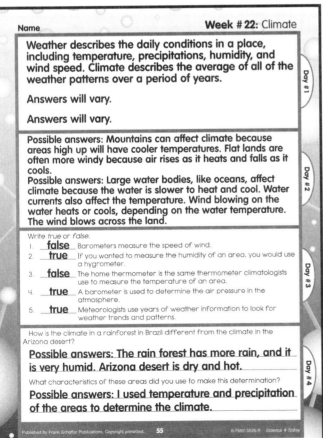

Weather describes the daily conditions in a place, including temperature, precipitations, humidity, and wind speed. Climate describes the average of all of the weather patterns over a period of years.

Answers will vary.

Answers will vary.

Day #1

Possible answers: Mountains can affect climate because areas high up will have cooler temperatures. Flat lands are often more windy because air rises as it heats and falls as it cools.
Possible answers: Large water bodies, like oceans, affect climate because the water is slower to heat and cool. Water currents also affect the temperature. Wind blowing on the water heats or cools, depending on the water temperature. The wind blows across the land.

Day #2

Write *true* or *false*.
1. **false** Barometers measure the speed of wind.
2. **true** If you wanted to measure the humidity of an area, you would use a hygrometer.
3. **false** The home thermometer is the same thermometer climatologists use to measure the temperature of an area.
4. **true** A barometer is used to determine the air pressure in the atmosphere.
5. **true** Meteorologists use years of weather information to look for weather trends and patterns.

Day #3

How is the climate in a rainforest in Brazil different from the climate in the Arizona desert?
Possible answers: The rain forest has more rain, and it is very humid. Arizona desert is dry and hot.

What characteristics of these areas did you use to make this determination?
Possible answers: I used temperature and precipitation of the areas to determine the climate.

Day #4

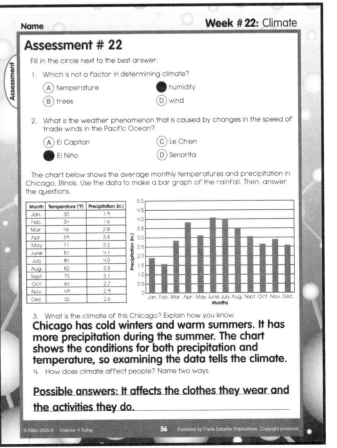

Assessment # 22

Fill in the circle next to the best answer.

1. Which is not a factor in determining climate?
   - (A) temperature
   - ● humidity
   - (B) trees
   - (D) wind

2. What is the weather phenomenon that is caused by changes in the speed of trade winds in the Pacific Ocean?
   - (A) El Capitan
   - (C) Le Chien
   - ● El Niño
   - (D) Senorita

The chart below shows the average monthly temperatures and precipitation in Chicago, Illinois. Use the data to make a bar graph of the rainfall. Then, answer the questions.

Month	Temperature (°F)	Precipitation (in.)
Jan.	30	1.9
Feb.	34	1.6
Mar.	46	2.8
Apr.	59	3.8
May	71	3.2
June	81	4.1
July	84	4.0
Aug.	82	3.5
Sept.	75	3.1
Oct.	64	2.7
Nov.	49	2.9
Dec.	35	2.6

3. What is the climate of this Chicago? Explain how you know.
Chicago has cold winters and warm summers. It has more precipitation during the summer. The chart shows the conditions for both precipitation and temperature, so examining the data tells the climate.

4. How does climate affect people? Name two ways.
Possible answers: It affects the clothes they wear and the activities they do.

Answer Key

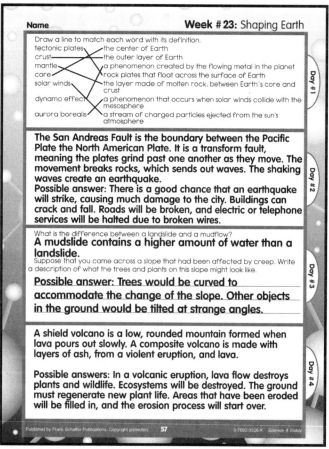

Day #1

Draw a line to match each word with its definition.

tectonic plates — rock plates that float across the surface of Earth
crust — the outer layer of Earth
mantle — the layer made of molten rock, between Earth's core and crust
core — the center of Earth
solar winds — a stream of charged particles ejected from the sun's atmosphere
dynamo effect — a phenomenon created by the flowing metal in the planet
aurora borealis — a phenomenon that occurs when solar winds collide with the mesosphere

Day #2

The San Andreas Fault is the boundary between the Pacific Plate the North American Plate. It is a transform fault, meaning the plates grind past one another as they move. The movement breaks rocks, which sends out waves. The shaking waves create an earthquake.

Possible answer: There is a good chance that an earthquake will strike, causing much damage to the city. Buildings can crack and fall. Roads will be broken, and electric or telephone services will be halted due to broken wires.

Day #3

What is the difference between a landslide and a mudflow?
A mudslide contains a higher amount of water than a landslide.

Suppose that you came across a slope that had been affected by creep. Write a description of what the trees and plants on this slope might look like.

Possible answer: Trees would be curved to accommodate the change of the slope. Other objects in the ground would be tilted at strange angles.

Day #4

A shield volcano is a low, rounded mountain formed when lava pours out slowly. A composite volcano is made with layers of ash, from a violent eruption, and lava.

Possible answers: In a volcanic eruption, lava flow destroys plants and wildlife. Ecosystems will be destroyed. The ground must regenerate new plant life. Areas that have been eroded will be filled in, and the erosion process will start over.

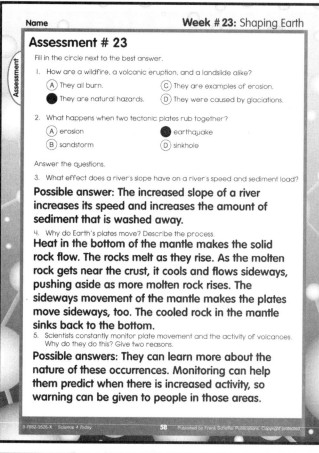

Assessment

Assessment # 23

Fill in the circle next to the best answer.

1. How are a wildfire, a volcanic eruption, and a landslide alike?
   - (A) They all burn.
   - (C) They are examples of erosion.
   - ● They are natural hazards.
   - (D) They were caused by glaciations.

2. What happens when two tectonic plates rub together?
   - (A) erosion
   - ● earthquake
   - (B) sandstorm
   - (D) sinkhole

Answer the questions.

3. What effect does a river's slope have on a river's speed and sediment load?

Possible answer: The increased slope of a river increases its speed and increases the amount of sediment that is washed away.

4. Why do Earth's plates move? Describe the process.

Heat in the bottom of the mantle makes the solid rock flow. The rocks melt as they rise. As the molten rock gets near the crust, it cools and flows sideways, pushing aside as more molten rock rises. The sideways movement of the mantle makes the plates move sideways, too. The cooled rock in the mantle sinks back to the bottom.

5. Scientists constantly monitor plate movement and the activity of volcanoes. Why do they do this? Give two reasons.

Possible answers: They can learn more about the nature of these occurrences. Monitoring can help them predict when there is increased activity, so warning can be given to people in those areas.

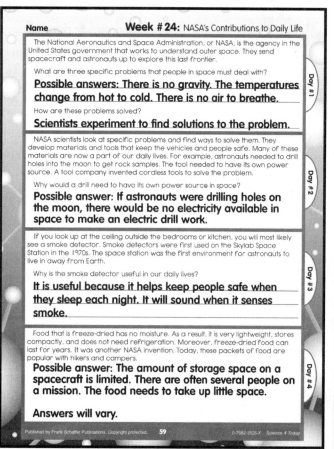

Day #1

The National Aeronautics and Space Administration, or NASA, is the agency in the United States government that works to understand outer space. They send spacecraft and astronauts up to explore this last frontier.

What are three specific problems that people in space must deal with?
Possible answers: There is no gravity. The temperatures change from hot to cold. There is no air to breathe.

How are these problems solved?
Scientists experiment to find solutions to the problem.

Day #2

NASA scientists look at specific problems and find ways to solve them. They develop materials and tools that keep the vehicles and people safe. Many of these materials are now a part of our daily lives. For example, astronauts needed to drill holes into the moon to get rock samples. The tool needed to have its own power source. A tool company invented cordless tools to solve the problem.

Why would a drill need to have its own power source in space?
Possible answer: If astronauts were drilling holes on the moon, there would be no electricity available in space to make an electric drill work.

Day #3

If you look up at the ceiling outside the bedrooms or kitchen, you will most likely see a smoke detector. Smoke detectors were first used on the Skylab Space Station in the 1970s. The space station was the first environment for astronauts to live in away from Earth.

Why is the smoke detector useful in our daily lives?
It is useful because it helps keep people safe when they sleep each night. It will sound when it senses smoke.

Day #4

Food that is freeze-dried has no moisture. As a result, it is very lightweight, stores compactly, and does not need refrigeration. Moreover, freeze-dried food can last for years. It was another NASA invention. Today, these packets of food are popular with hikers and campers.

Possible answer: The amount of storage space on a spacecraft is limited. There are often several people on a mission. The food needs to take up little space.

Answers will vary.

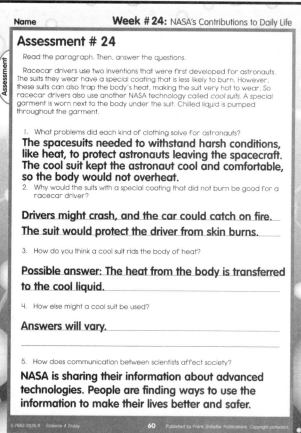

Assessment

Assessment # 24

Read the paragraph. Then, answer the questions.

Racecar drivers use two inventions that were first developed for astronauts. The suits they wear have a special coating that is less likely to burn. However, these suits can also trap the body's heat, making the suit very hot to wear. So racecar drivers also use another NASA technology called cool suits. A special garment is worn next to the body under the suit. Chilled liquid is pumped throughout the garment.

1. What problems did each kind of clothing solve for astronauts?
The spacesuits needed to withstand harsh conditions, like heat, to protect astronauts leaving the spacecraft. The cool suit kept the astronaut cool and comfortable, so the body would not overheat.

2. Why would the suits with a special coating that did not burn be good for a racecar driver?

Drivers might crash, and the car could catch on fire. The suit would protect the driver from skin burns.

3. How do you think a cool suit rids the body of heat?

Possible answer: The heat from the body is transferred to the cool liquid.

4. How else might a cool suit be used?

Answers will vary.

5. How does communication between scientists affect society?

NASA is sharing their information about advanced technologies. People are finding ways to use the information to make their lives better and safer.

Answer Key

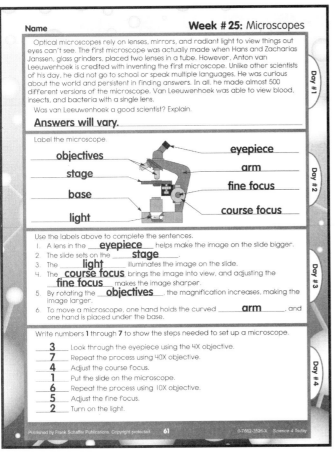

Day #1

Optical microscopes rely on lenses, mirrors, and radiant light to view things out eyes can't see. The first microscope was actually made when Hans and Zacharias Janssen, glass grinders, placed two lenses in a tube. However, Anton van Leeuwenhoek is credited with inventing the first microscope. Unlike other scientists of his day, he did not go to school or speak multiple languages. He was curious about the world and persistent in finding answers. In all, he made almost 500 different versions of the microscope. Van Leeuwenhoek was able to view blood, insects, and bacteria with a single lens.

Was van Leeuwenhoek a good scientist? Explain.

Answers will vary.

Day #2

Label the microscope.

objectives   eyepiece

stage   arm

base   fine focus

light   course focus

Day #3

Use the labels above to complete the sentences.

1. A lens in the **eyepiece** helps make the image on the slide bigger.
2. The slide sets on the **stage**.
3. The **light** illuminates the image on the slide.
4. The **course focus** brings the image into view, and adjusting the **fine focus** makes the image sharper.
5. By rotating the **objectives**, the magnification increases, making the image larger.
6. To move a microscope, one hand holds the curved **arm**, and one hand is placed under the base.

Day #4

Write numbers **1** through **7** to show the steps needed to set up a microscope.

   3   Look through the eyepiece using the 4X objective.
   7   Repeat the process using 40X objective.
   4   Adjust the course focus.
   1   Put the slide on the microscope.
   6   Repeat the process using 10X objective.
   5   Adjust the fine focus.
   2   Turn on the light.

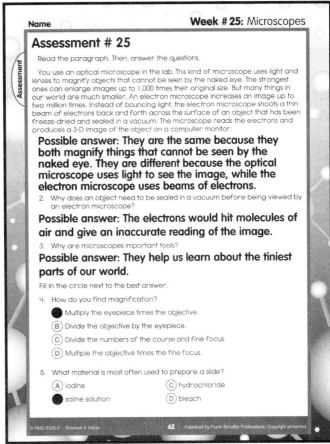

Assessment # 25

Read the paragraph. Then, answer the questions.

You use an optical microscope in the lab. This kind of microscope uses light and lenses to magnify objects that cannot be seen by the naked eye. The strongest ones can enlarge images up to 1,000 times their original size. But many things in our world are much smaller. An electron microscope increases an image up to two million times. Instead of bouncing light, the electron microscope shoots a thin beam of electrons back and forth across the surface of an object that has been freeze-dried and sealed in a vacuum. The microscope reads the electrons and produces a 3-D image of the object on a computer monitor.

Possible answer: They are the same because they both magnify things that cannot be seen by the naked eye. They are different because the optical microscope uses light to see the image, while the electron microscope uses beams of electrons.

2. Why does an object need to be sealed in a vacuum before being viewed by an electron microscope?

Possible answer: The electrons would hit molecules of air and give an inaccurate reading of the image.

3. Why are microscopes important tools?

Possible answer: They help us learn about the tiniest parts of our world.

Fill in the circle next to the best answer.

4. How do you find magnification?
   - ● Multiply the eyepiece times the objective.
   - Ⓑ Divide the objective by the eyepiece.
   - Ⓒ Divide the numbers of the course and fine focus.
   - Ⓓ Multiple the objective times the fine focus.

5. What material is most often used to prepare a slide?
   - Ⓐ iodine   Ⓒ hydrochloride
   - ● saline solution   Ⓓ bleach

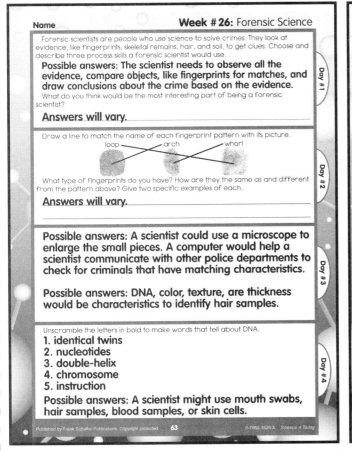

Day #1

Forensic scientists are people who use science to solve crimes. They look at evidence, like fingerprints, skeletal remains, hair, and soil, to get clues. Choose and describe three process skills a forensic scientist would use.

Possible answers: The scientist needs to observe all the evidence, compare objects, like fingerprints for matches, and draw conclusions about the crime based on the evidence.

What do you think would be the most interesting part of being a forensic scientist?

Answers will vary.

Day #2

Draw a line to match the name of each fingerprint pattern with its picture.

loop   arch   whorl

What type of fingerprints do you have? How are they the same as and different from the pattern above? Give two specific examples of each.

Answers will vary.

Day #3

Possible answers: A scientist could use a microscope to enlarge the small pieces. A computer would help a scientist communicate with other police departments to check for criminals that have matching characteristics.

Possible answers: DNA, color, texture, are thickness would be characteristics to identify hair samples.

Day #4

Unscramble the letters in bold to make words that tell about DNA.
1. **identical twins**
2. **nucleotides**
3. **double-helix**
4. **chromosome**
5. **instruction**

Possible answers: A scientist might use mouth swabs, hair samples, blood samples, or skin cells.

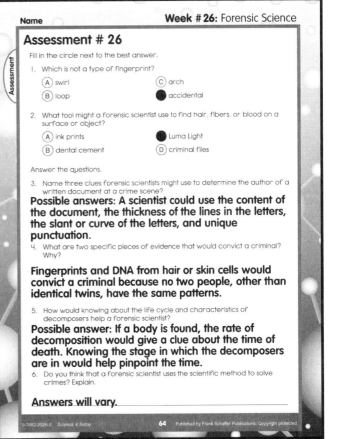

Assessment # 26

Fill in the circle next to the best answer.

1. Which is not a type of fingerprint?
   - Ⓐ swirl   Ⓒ arch
   - Ⓑ loop   ● accidental

2. What tool might a forensic scientist use to find hair, fibers, or blood on a surface or object?
   - Ⓐ ink prints   ● Luma Light
   - Ⓑ dental cement   Ⓓ criminal files

Answer the questions.

3. Name three clues forensic scientists might use to determine the author of a written document at a crime scene?

Possible answers: A scientist could use the content of the document, the thickness of the lines in the letters, the slant or curve of the letters, and unique punctuation.

4. What are two specific pieces of evidence that would convict a criminal? Why?

Fingerprints and DNA from hair or skin cells would convict a criminal because no two people, other than identical twins, have the same patterns.

5. How would knowing about the life cycle and characteristics of decomposers help a forensic scientist?

Possible answer: If a body is found, the rate of decomposition would give a clue about the time of death. Knowing the stage in which the decomposers are in would help pinpoint the time.

6. Do you think that a forensic scientist uses the scientific method to solve crimes? Explain.

Answers will vary.

Answer Key

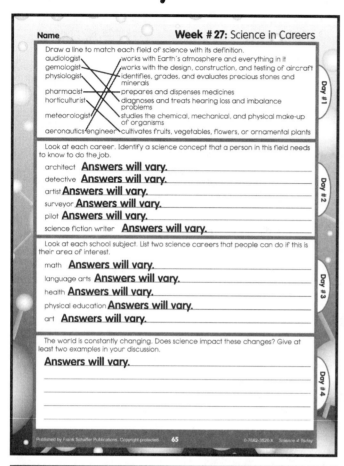

Name

Week # 27: Science in Careers

Day #1

Draw a line to match each field of science with its definition.

audiologist — works with Earth's atmosphere and everything in it

gemologist — works with the design, construction, and testing of aircraft

physiologist — identifies, grades, and evaluates precious stones and minerals

pharmacist — prepares and dispenses medicines

horticulturist — diagnoses and treats hearing loss and imbalance problems

meteorologist — studies the chemical, mechanical, and physical make-up of organisms

aeronautics engineer — cultivates fruits, vegetables, flowers, or ornamental plants

Day #2

Look at each career. Identify a science concept that a person in this field needs to know to do the job.

architect **Answers will vary.**

detective **Answers will vary.**

artist **Answers will vary.**

surveyor **Answers will vary.**

pilot **Answers will vary.**

science fiction writer **Answers will vary.**

Day #3

Look at each school subject. List two science careers that people can do if this is their area of interest.

math **Answers will vary.**

language arts **Answers will vary.**

health **Answers will vary.**

physical education **Answers will vary.**

art **Answers will vary.**

Day #4

The world is constantly changing. Does science impact these changes? Give at least two examples in your discussion.

Answers will vary.

Published by Frank Schaffer Publications. Copyright protected.   65   0-7682-3526-X   Science 4 Today

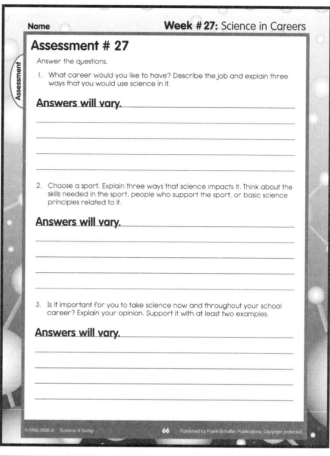

Name

Week # 27: Science in Careers

Assessment

Assessment # 27

Answer the questions.

1. What career would you like to have? Describe the job and explain three ways that you would use science in it.

Answers will vary.

2. Choose a sport. Explain three ways that science impacts it. Think about the skills needed in the sport, people who support the sport, or basic science principles related to it.

Answers will vary.

3. Is it important for you to take science now and throughout your school career? Explain your opinion. Support it with at least two examples.

Answers will vary.

0-7682-3526-X   Science 4 Today   66   Published by Frank Schaffer Publications. Copyright protected.

Name

Week # 28: Computer Use

Day #1

Possible answer: A computer's hardware includes its physical pieces, such as the monitor, keyboard, and mouse.

Possible answer: The software is the brain of the computer. It includes programs that make the computer function.

Possible answer: A document is the work you are creating in a software program.

Possible answer: The toolbar allows you to choose the font style, font size, margins, and other text features so that you can format the way a document looks.

Day #2

What are three reasons you use the Internet?

Answers will vary.

What are two benefits of e-mail?

Possible answers: You can communicate with people all around the world. You can contact people instantly.

Day #3

Complete each sentence to tell about a computer safety rule.

1. **Possible answer: your last name**
2. **Possible answer: you meet on the Internet**
3. **Possible answer: share them**
4. **Possible answer: virus protection**
5. **Possible answer: tell an adult**
6. **Possible answer: check with the person who owns the computer**

Day #4

Identify four computer programs and tell how you use them.

Answers will vary.

Published by Frank Schaffer Publications. Copyright protected.   67   0-7682-3526-X   Science 4 Today

---

Name

Week # 28: Computer Use

Assessment

Assessment # 28

Answer the questions.

1. Imagine that you are "chatting" online with a friend. Write a brief message telling about something that recently happened. Use the same language that you would type on the computer.

Answers will vary.

2. Now imagine that you are "chatting" online with an older family member. Would you use the same abbreviations, language, and words? Why or why not?

Answers will vary.

3. Why is it important to think about your audience before typing messages?

Possible answer: The message needs to be written to the age. An informal tone and language can be used with friends, but older people and those that are respected should receive messages having a more formal tone.

4. What are two positive and two negative aspects of computers in our society?

Answers will vary.

5. Think about all the places that use computers, including school, stores, transportation, and home. How do computers impact your daily life?

Answers will vary.

0-7682-3526-X   Science 4 Today   68   Published by Frank Schaffer Publications. Copyright protected.

Answer Key

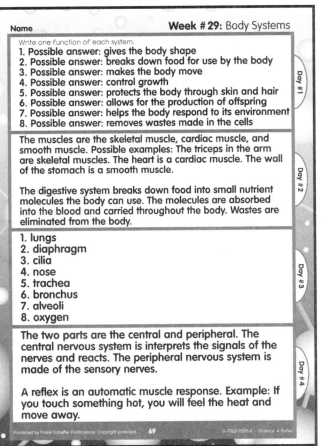

Week #29: Body Systems

Write one function of each system.
1. Possible answer: gives the body shape
2. Possible answer: breaks down food for use by the body
3. Possible answer: makes the body move
4. Possible answer: control growth
5. Possible answer: protects the body through skin and hair
6. Possible answer: allows for the production of offspring
7. Possible answer: helps the body respond to its environment
8. Possible answer: removes wastes made in the cells

Day #1

The muscles are the skeletal muscle, cardiac muscle, and smooth muscle. Possible examples: The triceps in the arm are skeletal muscles. The heart is a cardiac muscle. The wall of the stomach is a smooth muscle.

The digestive system breaks down food into small nutrient molecules the body can use. The molecules are absorbed into the blood and carried throughout the body. Wastes are eliminated from the body.

Day #2

1. lungs
2. diaphragm
3. cilia
4. nose
5. trachea
6. bronchus
7. alveoli
8. oxygen

Day #3

The two parts are the central and peripheral. The central nervous system is interprets the signals of the nerves and reacts. The peripheral nervous system is made of the sensory nerves.

A reflex is an automatic muscle response. Example: If you touch something hot, you will feel the heat and move away.

Day #4

Published by Frank Schaffer Publications. Copyright protected. 69   0-7682-3526-X   Science 4 Today

---

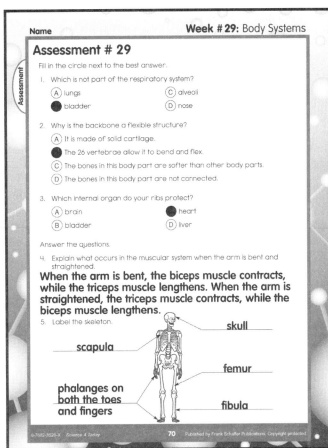

Week #29: Body Systems

Assessment # 29

Fill in the circle next to the best answer.

1. Which is not part of the respiratory system?
   - (A) lungs
   - (C) alveoli
   - ● bladder
   - (D) nose

2. Why is the backbone a flexible structure?
   - (A) It is made of solid cartilage.
   - ● The 26 vertebrae allow it to bend and flex.
   - (C) The bones in this body part are softer than other body parts.
   - (D) The bones in this body part are not connected.

3. Which internal organ do your ribs protect?
   - (A) brain
   - ● heart
   - (B) bladder
   - (D) liver

Answer the questions.

4. Explain what occurs in the muscular system when the arm is bent and straightened.

When the arm is bent, the biceps muscle contracts, while the triceps muscle lengthens. When the arm is straightened, the triceps muscle contracts, while the biceps muscle lengthens.

5. Label the skeleton.

skull

scapula

femur

phalanges on both the toes and fingers

fibula

0-7682-3526-X   Science 4 Today   70   Published by Frank Schaffer Publications. Copyright protected.

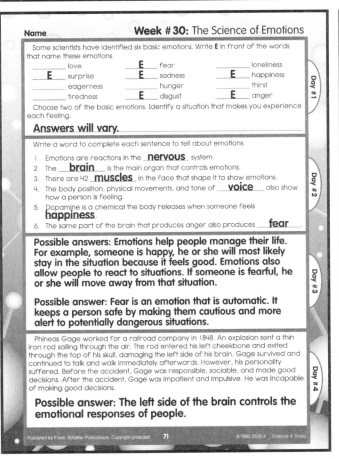

Week #30: The Science of Emotions

Some scientists have identified six basic emotions. Write **E** in front of the words that name these emotions.

____ love   **E** fear   ____ loneliness
E surprise   **E** sadness   **E** happiness
____ eagerness   ____ hunger   ____ thirst
____ tiredness   **E** disgust   **E** anger

Choose two of the basic emotions. Identify a situation that makes you experience each feeling.

Answers will vary.

Day #1

Write a word to complete each sentence to tell about emotions.
1. Emotions are reactions in the **nervous** system.
2. The **brain** is the main organ that controls emotions.
3. There are 42 **muscles** in the face that shape it to show emotions.
4. The body position, physical movements, and tone of **voice** also show how a person is feeling.
5. Dopamine is a chemical the body releases when someone feels **happiness**.
6. The same part of the brain that produces anger also produces **fear**.

Day #2

Possible answers: Emotions help people manage their life. For example, someone is happy, he or she will most likely stay in the situation because it feels good. Emotions also allow people to react to situations. If someone is fearful, he or she will move away from that situation.

Possible answer: Fear is an emotion that is automatic. It keeps a person safe by making them cautious and more alert to potentially dangerous situations.

Day #3

Phineas Gage worked for a railroad company in 1848. An explosion sent a thin iron rod sailing through the air. The rod entered his left cheekbone and exited through the top of his skull, damaging the left side of his brain. Gage survived and continued to talk and walk immediately afterwards. However, his personality suffered. Before the accident, Gage was responsible, sociable, and made good decisions. After the accident, Gage was impatient and impulsive. He was incapable of making good decisions.

Possible answer: The left side of the brain controls the emotional responses of people.

Day #4

Published by Frank Schaffer Publications. Copyright protected. 71   0-7682-3526-X   Science 4 Today

---

Week #30: The Science of Emotions

Assessment # 30

Answer the questions.

1. Do you think people can fake emotions? Explain.

Answers will vary.

2. Can emotions affect the health of your body? Explain.
Possible answer: Yes, emotions can affect the health of the body. Feeling continuous stress and fear can cause long-term health issues, including heart and digestive problems.

3. Extreme emotions can happen when a person is not physically or mentally healthy. For example, depression is the extreme emotion of sadness. How might drug and alcohol abuse be the result of the extreme happiness?
Drugs and alcohol affect the brain, often giving the user a sense of extreme pleasure, happiness, and wellbeing. People may use the drug more frequently or in larger doses to maintain that happy feeling.

4. Darria has a friend who has been acting differently. She has not been eating as much and is avoiding her friends. What should Darria do?

Answers will vary.

Fill in the circle next the best answer.

5. What happens to the body when a person feels fear?
   - ● The heart beats faster.
   - (C) The body gets sleepy.
   - (B) The arm muscles relax.
   - (D) The body temperature increases.

6. Which is not a process of the brain in response to an emotion?
   - (A) react
   - (C) recognize
   - (B) show
   - ● ignore

0-7682-3526-X   Science 4 Today   72   Published by Frank Schaffer Publications. Copyright protected.

Answer Key

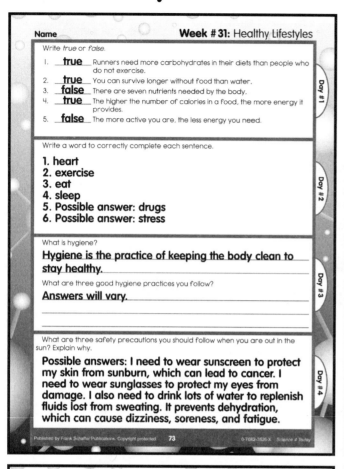

Day #1

Write *true* or *false*.

1. **true** Runners need more carbohydrates in their diets than people who do not exercise.
2. **true** You can survive longer without food than water.
3. **false** There are seven nutrients needed by the body.
4. **true** The higher the number of calories in a food, the more energy it provides.
5. **false** The more active you are, the less energy you need.

Day #2

Write a word to correctly complete each sentence.

1. heart
2. exercise
3. eat
4. sleep
5. Possible answer: drugs
6. Possible answer: stress

Day #3

What is hygiene?

Hygiene is the practice of keeping the body clean to stay healthy.

What are three good hygiene practices you follow?

Answers will vary.

Day #4

What are three safety precautions you should follow when you are out in the sun? Explain why.

Possible answers: I need to wear sunscreen to protect my skin from sunburn, which can lead to cancer. I need to wear sunglasses to protect my eyes from damage. I also need to drink lots of water to replenish fluids lost from sweating. It prevents dehydration, which can cause dizziness, soreness, and fatigue.

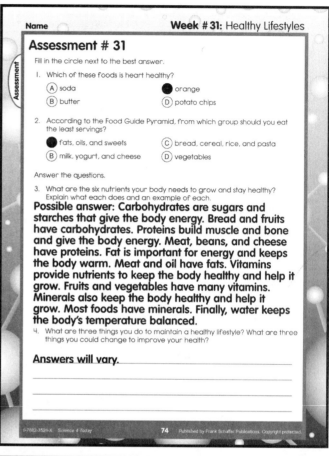

Assessment

Assessment # 31

Fill in the circle next to the best answer.

1. Which of these foods is heart healthy?
   - (A) soda
   - ● orange
   - (B) butter
   - (D) potato chips

2. According to the Food Guide Pyramid, from which group should you eat the least servings?
   - ● fats, oils, and sweets
   - (C) bread, cereal, rice, and pasta
   - (B) milk, yogurt, and cheese
   - (D) vegetables

Answer the questions.

3. What are the six nutrients your body needs to grow and stay healthy? Explain what each does and an example of each.

Possible answer: Carbohydrates are sugars and starches that give the body energy. Bread and fruits have carbohydrates. Proteins build muscle and bone and give the body energy. Meat, beans, and cheese have proteins. Fat is important for energy and keeps the body warm. Meat and oil have fats. Vitamins provide nutrients to keep the body healthy and help it grow. Fruits and vegetables have many vitamins. Minerals also keep the body healthy and help it grow. Most foods have minerals. Finally, water keeps the body's temperature balanced.

4. What are three things you do to maintain a healthy lifestyle? What are three things you could change to improve your health?

Answers will vary.

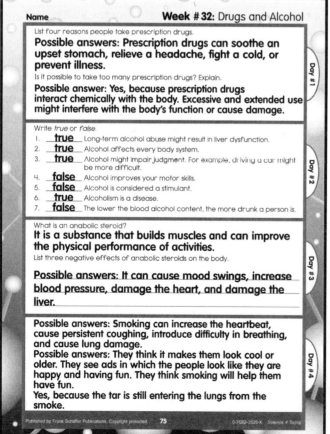

Day #1

List four reasons people take prescription drugs.

Possible answers: Prescription drugs can soothe an upset stomach, relieve a headache, fight a cold, or prevent illness.

Is it possible to take too many prescription drugs? Explain.

Possible answer: Yes, because prescription drugs interact chemically with the body. Excessive and extended use might interfere with the body's function or cause damage.

Day #2

Write *true* or *false*.

1. **true** Long-term alcohol abuse might result in liver dysfunction.
2. **true** Alcohol affects every body system.
3. **true** Alcohol might impair judgment. For example, driving a car might be more difficult.
4. **false** Alcohol improves your motor skills.
5. **false** Alcohol is considered a stimulant.
6. **true** Alcoholism is a disease.
7. **false** The lower the blood alcohol content, the more drunk a person is.

Day #3

What is an anabolic steroid?

It is a substance that builds muscles and can improve the physical performance of activities.

List three negative effects of anabolic steroids on the body.

Possible answers: It can cause mood swings, increase blood pressure, damage the heart, and damage the liver.

Day #4

Possible answers: Smoking can increase the heartbeat, cause persistent coughing, introduce difficulty in breathing, and cause lung damage.
Possible answers: They think it makes them look cool or older. They see ads in which the people look like they are happy and having fun. They think smoking will help them have fun.
Yes, because the tar is still entering the lungs from the smoke.

Assessment

Assessment # 32

Fill in the circle next to the best answer.

1. Which is a not an effect of alcohol?
   - (A) blurred vision
   - ● improved muscle coordination
   - (B) impaired ability to make decisions
   - (D) changes in mood

2. Which is not an effect of inhalants?
   - ● sleepiness
   - (C) difficulty breathing
   - (B) headaches
   - (D) nervousness

3. Imagine that a friend has told you that she is thinking about taking diet pills to increase her energy level and to lose some weight. You know that the pills she is describing are really amphetamines. What will you tell your friend? Write a paragraph arguing against the use of these pills. Use what you know about drugs and the importance of a healthy lifestyle to persuade her to stay away from diet pills.

Answers will vary.

4. Explain the effect that stimulants have on the nervous system.

Possible answers: The heart rate increases, breathing becomes more rapid, there is nervousness and paranoia.

5. Why do you think over-the-counter drugs and prescription drugs are sold in a pharmacy?

Answers will vary.

Answer Key

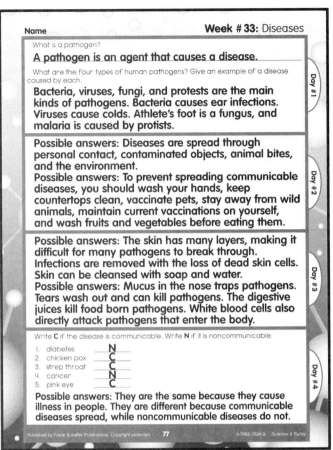

Name _____ **Week #33:** Diseases

What is a pathogen?

A pathogen is an agent that causes a disease.

What are the four types of human pathogens? Give an example of a disease caused by each.

Bacteria, viruses, fungi, and protests are the main kinds of pathogens. Bacteria causes ear infections. Viruses cause colds. Athlete's foot is a fungus, and malaria is caused by protists.

Day #1

Possible answers: Diseases are spread through personal contact, contaminated objects, animal bites, and the environment.
Possible answers: To prevent spreading communicable diseases, you should wash your hands, keep countertops clean, vaccinate pets, stay away from wild animals, maintain current vaccinations on yourself, and wash fruits and vegetables before eating them.

Day #2

Possible answers: The skin has many layers, making it difficult for many pathogens to break through. Infections are removed with the loss of dead skin cells. Skin can be cleansed with soap and water.
Possible answers: Mucus in the nose traps pathogens. Tears wash out and can kill pathogens. The digestive juices kill food born pathogens. White blood cells also directly attack pathogens that enter the body.

Day #3

Write **C** if the disease is communicable. Write **N** if it is noncommunicable.

1. diabetes _____ **N**
2. chicken pox _____ **C**
3. strep throat _____ **C**
4. cancer _____ **N**
5. pink eye _____ **C**

Possible answers: They are the same because they cause illness in people. They are different because communicable diseases spread, while noncommunicable diseases do not.

Day #4

Published by Frank Schaffer Publications. Copyright protected.   77   0-7682-3526-X Science 4 Today

---

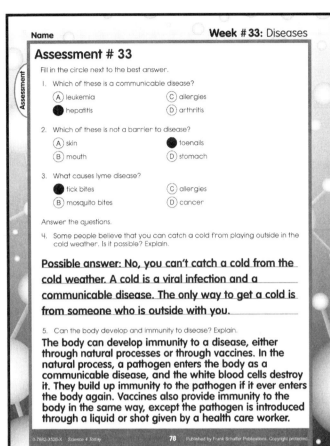

Name _____ **Week #33:** Diseases

Assessment # 33

Assessment

Fill in the circle next to the best answer.

1. Which of these is a communicable disease?
   - (A) leukemia
   - (C) allergies
   - ● hepatitis
   - (D) arthritis

2. Which of these is not a barrier to disease?
   - (A) skin
   - ● toenails
   - (B) mouth
   - (D) stomach

3. What causes lyme disease?
   - ● tick bites
   - (C) allergies
   - (B) mosquito bites
   - (D) cancer

Answer the questions.

4. Some people believe that you can catch a cold from playing outside in the cold weather. Is it possible? Explain.

Possible answer: No, you can't catch a cold from the cold weather. A cold is a viral infection and a communicable disease. The only way to get a cold is from someone who is outside with you.

5. Can the body develop and immunity to disease? Explain.

The body can develop immunity to a disease, either through natural processes or through vaccines. In the natural process, a pathogen enters the body as a communicable disease, and the white blood cells destroy it. They build up immunity to the pathogen if it ever enters the body again. Vaccines also provide immunity to the body in the same way, except the pathogen is introduced through a liquid or shot given by a health care worker.

0-7682-3526-X Science 4 Today   78   Published by Frank Schaffer Publications. Copyright protected.

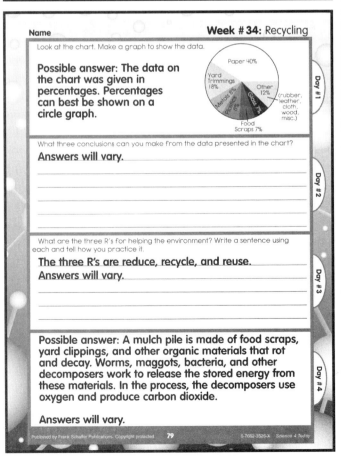

Name _____ **Week #34:** Recycling

Look at the chart. Make a graph to show the data.

Possible answer: The data on the chart was given in percentages. Percentages can best be shown on a circle graph.

Paper 40%
Yard Trimmings 18%
Other 12% (rubber, leather, cloth, wood, misc.)
Metals 8%
Plastics 8%
Glass 7%
Food Scraps 7%

Day #1

What three conclusions can you make from the data presented in the chart?

Answers will vary. _____

Day #2

What are the three R's for helping the environment? Write a sentence using each and tell how you practice it.

The three R's are reduce, recycle, and reuse.
Answers will vary. _____

Day #3

Possible answer: A mulch pile is made of food scraps, yard clippings, and other organic materials that rot and decay. Worms, maggots, bacteria, and other decomposers work to release the stored energy from these materials. In the process, the decomposers use oxygen and produce carbon dioxide.

Answers will vary.

Day #4

Published by Frank Schaffer Publications. Copyright protected.   79   0-7682-3526-X Science 4 Today

---

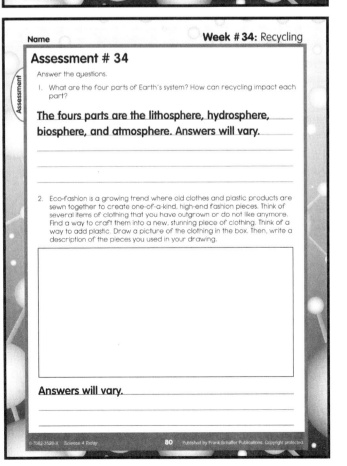

Name _____ **Week #34:** Recycling

Assessment # 34

Assessment

Answer the questions.

1. What are the four parts of Earth's system? How can recycling impact each part?

The fours parts are the lithosphere, hydrosphere, biosphere, and atmosphere. Answers will vary.

2. Eco-fashion is a growing trend where old clothes and plastic products are sewn together to create one-of-a-kind, high-end fashion pieces. Think of several items of clothing that you have outgrown or do not like anymore. Find a way to craft them into a new, stunning piece of clothing. Think of a way to add plastic. Draw a picture of the clothing in the box. Then, write a description of the pieces you used in your drawing.

Answers will vary. _____

0-7682-3526-X Science 4 Today   80   Published by Frank Schaffer Publications. Copyright protected.

Answer Key

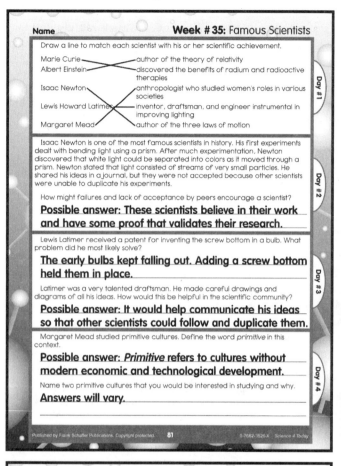

Name   **Week #35:** Famous Scientists

Draw a line to match each scientist with his or her scientific achievement.

Marie Curie — discovered the benefits of radium and radioactive therapies

Albert Einstein — author of the theory of relativity

Isaac Newton — anthropologist who studied women's roles in various societies

Lewis Howard Latimer — inventor, draftsman, and engineer instrumental in improving lighting

Margaret Mead — author of the three laws of motion

(Day #1)

Isaac Newton is one of the most famous scientists in history. His first experiments dealt with bending light using a prism. After much experimentation, Newton discovered that white light could be separated into colors as it moved through a prism. Newton stated that light consisted of streams of very small particles. He shared his ideas in a journal, but they were not accepted because other scientists were unable to duplicate his experiments.

How might failures and lack of acceptance by peers encourage a scientist?

Possible answer: These scientists believe in their work and have some proof that validates their research.

(Day #2)

Lewis Latimer received a patent for inventing the screw bottom in a bulb. What problem did he most likely solve?

The early bulbs kept falling out. Adding a screw bottom held them in place.

Latimer was a very talented draftsman. He made careful drawings and diagrams of all his ideas. How would this be helpful in the scientific community?

Possible answer: It would help communicate his ideas so that other scientists could follow and duplicate them.

(Day #3)

Margaret Mead studied primitive cultures. Define the word *primitive* in this context.

Possible answer: *Primitive* refers to cultures without modern economic and technological development.

Name two primitive cultures that you would be interested in studying and why.

Answers will vary.

(Day #4)

Published by Frank Schaffer Publications. Copyright protected.   81   0-7682-3526-X   *Science 4 Today*

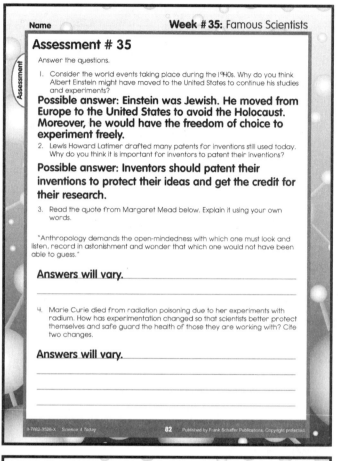

Name   **Week #35:** Famous Scientists

Assessment #35

Answer the questions.

1. Consider the world events taking place during the 1940s. Why do you think Albert Einstein might have moved to the United States to continue his studies and experiments?

Possible answer: Einstein was Jewish. He moved from Europe to the United States to avoid the Holocaust. Moreover, he would have the freedom of choice to experiment freely.

2. Lewis Howard Latimer drafted many patents for inventions still used today. Why do you think it is important for inventors to patent their inventions?

Possible answer: Inventors should patent their inventions to protect their ideas and get the credit for their research.

3. Read the quote from Margaret Mead below. Explain it using your own words.

"Anthropology demands the open-mindedness with which one must look and listen, record in astonishment and wonder that which one would not have been able to guess."

Answers will vary.

4. Marie Curie died from radiation poisoning due to her experiments with radium. How has experimentation changed so that scientists better protect themselves and safe guard the health of those they are working with? Cite two changes.

Answers will vary.

(Assessment)

0-7682-3526-X   *Science 4 Today*   82   Published by Frank Schaffer Publications. Copyright protected.

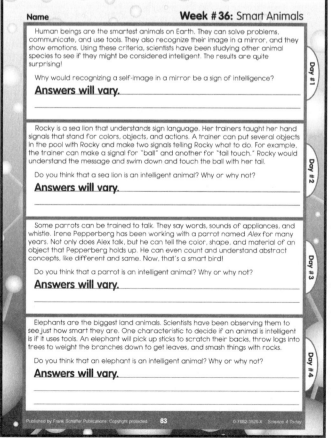

Name   **Week #36:** Smart Animals

Human beings are the smartest animals on Earth. They can solve problems, communicate, and use tools. They also recognize their image in a mirror, and they show emotions. Using these criteria, scientists have been studying other animal species to see if they might be considered intelligent. The results are quite surprising!

Why would recognizing a self-image in a mirror be a sign of intelligence?

Answers will vary.

(Day #1)

Rocky is a sea lion that understands sign language. Her trainers taught her hand signals that stand for colors, objects, and actions. A trainer can put several objects in the pool with Rocky and make two signals telling Rocky what to do. For example, the trainer can make a signal for "ball" and another for "tail touch." Rocky would understand the message and swim down and touch the ball with her tail.

Do you think that a sea lion is an intelligent animal? Why or why not?

Answers will vary.

(Day #2)

Some parrots can be trained to talk. They say words, sounds of appliances, and whistle. Irene Pepperberg has been working with a parrot named *Alex* for many years. Not only does Alex talk, but he can tell the color, shape, and material of an object that Pepperberg holds up. He can even count and understand abstract concepts, like different and same. Now, that's a smart bird!

Do you think that a parrot is an intelligent animal? Why or why not?

Answers will vary.

(Day #3)

Elephants are the biggest land animals. Scientists have been observing them to see just how smart they are. One characteristic to decide if an animal is intelligent is if it uses tools. An elephant will pick up sticks to scratch their backs, throw logs into trees to weight the branches down to get leaves, and smash things with rocks.

Do you think that an elephant is an intelligent animal? Why or why not?

Answers will vary.

(Day #4)

Published by Frank Schaffer Publications. Copyright protected.   83   0-7682-3526-X   *Science 4 Today*

Name   **Week #36:** Smart Animals

Assessment #36

Read the paragraph. Then, answer the questions.

Chimpanzees are the closest relatives to human beings because of their chemical make-up and physical structure. Increased research shows they also exhibit many characteristics of intelligence. They are very social animals that live in large groups. Jane Goodall, a naturalist, spent many years in Africa studying the animals in the wild. Goodall observed that the chimps used their voices, faces, and hands to tell others how they felt. They fished ants out of the ground with blades of grass and opened nuts with rocks. Amazingly, they fought other troops of monkeys, swinging sticks as clubs to kill each other. Moreover, Goodall saw their emotions. One chimp was so upset about the death of his mother that he stopped eating and died, too.

1. According to the article, what are three ways that scientists judge the intelligence of chimps? Explain.

They have emotions, like sadness when a group member dies. They communicate these feelings with their voices, faces, and hands. They use tools, like rocks to open nuts.

2. Why is it important to learn about animals? How does the information help us learn more about human beings?

Answers will vary.

3. What three process skills can a scientist use when working with animals? Explain their use.

Possible answers: They can observe to see how an animal acts. They can experiment with different ways to teach animals skills. They can communicate with the animals and with other scientists.

4. Some animal rights groups believe that is unethical to experiment and work with animals. Why? What is your opinion?

Answers will vary.

(Assessment)

0-7682-3526-X   *Science 4 Today*   84   Published by Frank Schaffer Publications. Copyright protected.

0-7682-3526-X   *Science 4 Today*   **110**   Published by Frank Schaffer Publications. Copyright protected.

Answer Key

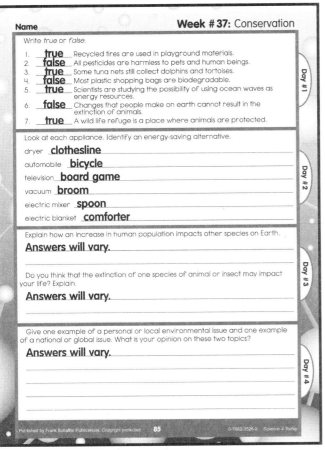

Day #1

Write *true* or *false*.

1. **true** Recycled tires are used in playground materials.
2. **false** All pesticides are harmless to pets and human beings.
3. **true** Some tuna nets still collect dolphins and tortoises.
4. **false** Most plastic shopping bags are biodegradable.
5. **true** Scientists are studying the possibility of using ocean waves as energy resources.
6. **false** Changes that people make on earth cannot result in the extinction of animals.
7. **true** A wild life refuge is a place where animals are protected.

Day #2

Look at each appliance. Identify an energy-saving alternative.

dryer **clothesline**
automobile **bicycle**
television **board game**
vacuum **broom**
electric mixer **spoon**
electric blanket **comforter**

Day #3

Explain how an increase in human population impacts other species on Earth.

Answers will vary.

Do you think that the extinction of one species of animal or insect may impact your life? Explain.

Answers will vary.

Day #4

Give one example of a personal or local environmental issue and one example of a national or global issue. What is your opinion on these two topics?

Answers will vary.

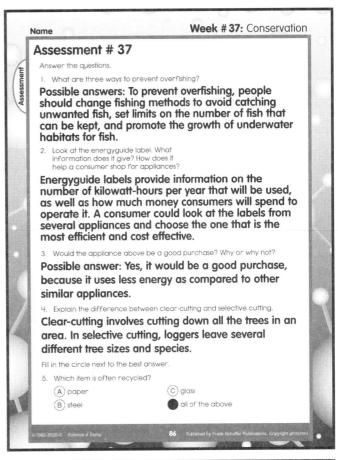

Assessment

Assessment # 37

Answer the questions.

1. What are three ways to prevent overfishing?

Possible answers: To prevent overfishing, people should change fishing methods to avoid catching unwanted fish, set limits on the number of fish that can be kept, and promote the growth of underwater habitats for fish.

2. Look at the energyguide label. What information does it give? How does it help a consumer shop for appliances?

Energyguide labels provide information on the number of kilowatt-hours per year that will be used, as well as how much money consumers will spend to operate it. A consumer could look at the labels from several appliances and choose the one that is the most efficient and cost effective.

3. Would the appliance above be a good purchase? Why or why not?

Possible answer: Yes, it would be a good purchase, because it uses less energy as compared to other similar appliances.

4. Explain the difference between clear-cutting and selective cutting.

Clear-cutting involves cutting down all the trees in an area. In selective cutting, loggers leave several different tree sizes and species.

Fill in the circle next to the best answer.

5. Which item is often recycled?
   - (A) paper
   - (B) steel
   - (C) glass
   - ● all of the above

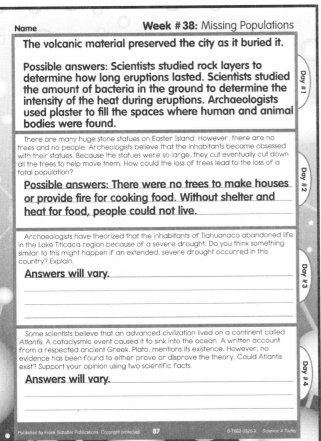

Day #1

The volcanic material preserved the city as it buried it.

Possible answers: Scientists studied rock layers to determine how long eruptions lasted. Scientists studied the amount of bacteria in the ground to determine the intensity of the heat during eruptions. Archaeologists used plaster to fill the spaces where human and animal bodies were found.

Day #2

There are many huge stone statues on Easter Island. However, there are no trees and no people. Archaeologists believe that the inhabitants became obsessed with their statues. Because the statues were so large, they cut eventually cut down all the trees to help move them. How could the loss of trees lead to the loss of a total population?

Possible answers: There were no trees to make houses or provide fire for cooking food. Without shelter and heat for food, people could not live.

Day #3

Archaeologists have theorized that the inhabitants of Tiahuanaco abandoned life in the Lake Titicaca region because of a severe drought. Do you think something similar to this might happen if an extended, severe drought occurred in this country? Explain.

Answers will vary.

Day #4

Some scientists believe that an advanced civilization lived on a continent called *Atlantis*. A cataclysmic event caused it to sink into the ocean. A written account from a respected ancient Greek, Plato, mentions its existence. However, no evidence has been found to either prove or disprove the theory. Could Atlantis exist? Support your opinion using two scientific facts.

Answers will vary.

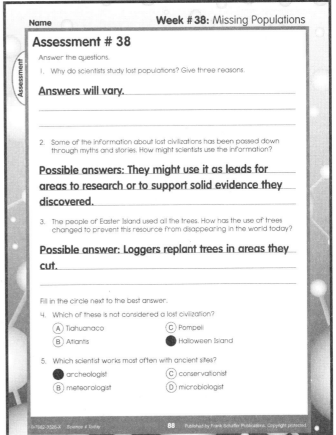

Assessment

Assessment # 38

Answer the questions.

1. Why do scientists study lost populations? Give three reasons.

Answers will vary.

2. Some of the information about lost civilizations has been passed down through myths and stories. How might scientists use the information?

Possible answers: They might use it as leads for areas to research or to support solid evidence they discovered.

3. The people of Easter Island used all the trees. How has the use of trees changed to prevent this resource from disappearing in the world today?

Possible answer: Loggers replant trees in areas they cut.

Fill in the circle next to the best answer.

4. Which of these is not considered a lost civilization?
   - (A) Tiahuanaco
   - (B) Atlantis
   - (C) Pompeii
   - ● Halloween Island

5. Which scientist works most often with ancient sites?
   - ● archeologist
   - (B) meteorologist
   - (C) conservationist
   - (D) microbiologist

Answer Key

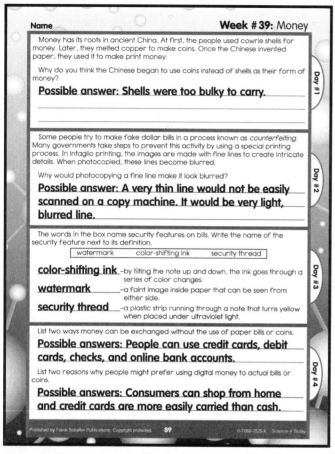

Money has its roots in ancient China. At first, the people used cowrie shells for money. Later, they melted copper to make coins. Once the Chinese invented paper, they used it to make print money.

Why do you think the Chinese began to use coins instead of shells as their form of money?

Possible answer: Shells were too bulky to carry.

Day #1

Some people try to make fake dollar bills in a process known as *counterfeiting*. Many governments take steps to prevent this activity by using a special printing process. In intaglio printing, the images are made with fine lines to create intricate details. When photocopied, these lines become blurred.

Why would photocopying a fine line make it look blurred?

Possible answer: A very thin line would not be easily scanned on a copy machine. It would be very light, blurred line.

Day #2

The words in the box name security features on bills. Write the name of the security feature next to its definition.

| watermark | color-shifting ink | security thread |

color-shifting ink –by tilting the note up and down, the ink goes through a series of color changes.

watermark –a faint image inside paper that can be seen from either side.

security thread –a plastic strip running through a note that turns yellow when placed under ultraviolet light.

Day #3

List two ways money can be exchanged without the use of paper bills or coins.

Possible answers: People can use credit cards, debit cards, checks, and online bank accounts.

List two reasons why people might prefer using digital money to actual bills or coins.

Possible answers: Consumers can shop from home and credit cards are more easily carried than cash.

Day #4

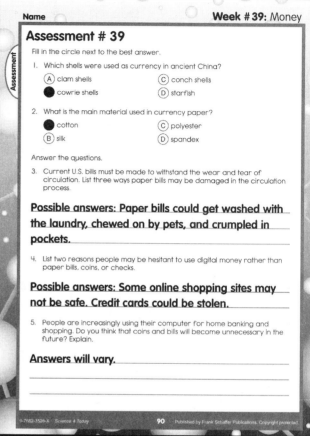

Assessment

Assessment # 39

Fill in the circle next to the best answer.

1. Which shells were used as currency in ancient China?
   - (A) clam shells
   - (C) conch shells
   - ● cowrie shells
   - (D) starfish

2. What is the main material used in currency paper?
   - ● cotton
   - (C) polyester
   - (B) silk
   - (D) spandex

Answer the questions.

3. Current U.S. bills must be made to withstand the wear and tear of circulation. List three ways paper bills may be damaged in the circulation process.

Possible answers: Paper bills could get washed with the laundry, chewed on by pets, and crumpled in pockets.

4. List two reasons people may be hesitant to use digital money rather than paper bills, coins, or checks.

Possible answers: Some online shopping sites may not be safe. Credit cards could be stolen.

5. People are increasingly using their computer for home banking and shopping. Do you think that coins and bills will become unnecessary in the future? Explain.

Answers will vary.

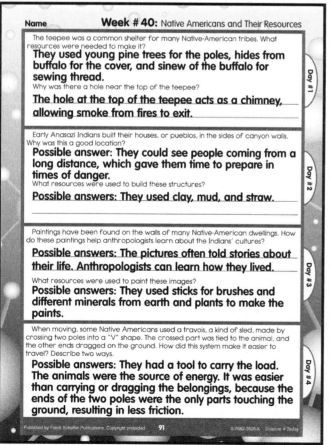

The teepee was a common shelter for many Native-American tribes. What resources were needed to make it?

They used young pine trees for the poles, hides from buffalo for the cover, and sinew of the buffalo for sewing thread.

Why was there a hole near the top of the teepee?

The hole at the top of the teepee acts as a chimney, allowing smoke from fires to exit.

Day #1

Early Anasazi Indians built their houses, or pueblos, in the sides of canyon walls. Why was this a good location?

Possible answer: They could see people coming from a long distance, which gave them time to prepare in times of danger.

What resources were used to build these structures?

Possible answers: They used clay, mud, and straw.

Day #2

Paintings have been found on the walls of many Native-American dwellings. How do these paintings help anthropologists learn about the Indians' cultures?

Possible answers: The pictures often told stories about their life. Anthropologists can learn how they lived.

What resources were used to paint these images?

Possible answers: They used sticks for brushes and different minerals from earth and plants to make the paints.

Day #3

When moving, some Native Americans used a travois, a kind of sled, made by crossing two poles into a "V" shape. The crossed part was tied to the animal, and the other ends dragged on the ground. How did this system make it easier to travel? Describe two ways.

Possible answers: They had a tool to carry the load. The animals were the source of energy. It was easier than carrying or dragging the belongings, because the ends of the two poles were the only parts touching the ground, resulting in less friction.

Day #4

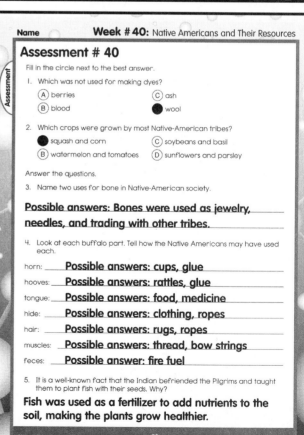

Assessment

Assessment # 40

Fill in the circle next to the best answer.

1. Which was not used for making dyes?
   - (A) berries
   - (C) ash
   - (B) blood
   - ● wool

2. Which crops were grown by most Native-American tribes?
   - ● squash and corn
   - (C) soybeans and basil
   - (B) watermelon and tomatoes
   - (D) sunflowers and parsley

Answer the questions.

3. Name two uses for bone in Native-American society.

Possible answers: Bones were used as jewelry, needles, and trading with other tribes.

4. Look at each buffalo part. Tell how the Native Americans may have used each.

horn: **Possible answers: cups, glue**

hooves: **Possible answers: rattles, glue**

tongue: **Possible answers: food, medicine**

hide: **Possible answers: clothing, ropes**

hair: **Possible answers: rugs, ropes**

muscles: **Possible answers: thread, bow strings**

feces: **Possible answer: fire fuel**

5. It is a well-known fact that the Indian befriended the Pilgrims and taught them to plant fish with their seeds. Why?

Fish was used as a fertilizer to add nutrients to the soil, making the plants grow healthier.
